POPULATION
MOVEMENTS

THREE PUBLIC LECTURES GIVEN
AT THE UNIVERSITY OF LONDON
MARCH 1936

POPULATION
MOVEMENTS

BY

ROBERT R. KUCZYNSKI

Department of Social Biology
London School of Economics

OXFORD
AT THE CLARENDON PRESS
1936

OXFORD UNIVERSITY PRESS
AMEN HOUSE, E.C. 4
London Edinburgh Glasgow New York
Toronto Melbourne Capetown Bombay
Calcutta Madras
HUMPHREY MILFORD
PUBLISHER TO THE UNIVERSITY

PRINTED IN GREAT BRITAIN

CONTENTS

I

II

III

I

i. Our Knowledge of the Population of the Earth

WHEN the House of Commons in 1825 presented an address to His Majesty praying that he would be graciously pleased to order certain information to be laid before them relative to the population of the Cape of Good Hope, communications were so slow that it took eight or nine months before the desired data on births and deaths by races reached London. If to-day the House of Commons made a similar request, it could be cabled to Pretoria, and the reply might be here the next day. But it would read: Sorry; compulsory birth and death registration of non-Europeans was abolished in 1924 for all rural areas. We now have good communications, but we have not much to communicate.

South Africa is not the only example of this kind. If you want to know the births and deaths by races in French West Africa, say, for 1835, you will find ample information in the *Annales maritimes et coloniales*. If you desire similar figures for recent times you will be told that the superstitions of the natives present unsurmountable difficulties to the collection of such data.

For England, you can compare the number of

births by sex and legitimacy for each year from 1842 to 1934. But you can do no more. You have here no retrogression as in South or West Africa, but you do have stagnation. While many countries in Europe, while Canada, Australia, and New Zealand publish the number of births according to the age of parents, the order of births, &c., yet all these data are lacking for England. This inadequacy of English birth statistics is not only a serious impediment in the study of fertility; but it also makes it impossible to appraise rightly the trend of maternal mortality. Maternal mortality is particularly high in the case of first children. If you cannot relate the number of deaths in first childbed to the total number of first-born, the number of deaths in second childbed to the total number of second-born, &c., you cannot tell whether the recent trend of maternal mortality has been favourable or not.

But retrogression or stagnation in vital statistics are, even so, only exceptions, and most countries which collected such statistics in earlier times have improved upon them since. Progress has been achieved also inasmuch as the number of countries with no vital statistics at all has diminished notably. One hundred years ago Belgium, France, Austria, some German States, and the Scandinavian countries were the only countries in Europe which collected birth and death statistics. To-day Albania is the only country which does not do so. The gaps are likewise insignificant in North America. They are more serious in Central America and Oceania, they comprise about three-fifths of the population of South America and Asia, and about four-fifths of the population of Africa. The countries without vital statistics account perhaps for two-fifths of the population of the earth. But this does not imply that we have a fair knowledge of recent births and deaths for three-fifths of the population of the earth. No vital statistics have been published for Soviet Russia since 1929. In numerous other countries vital statistics are by no means complete. If we include only those countries for which vital statistics have been published since 1929 or for which the published numbers of both births and deaths can safely be said not to lag behind the actual numbers by more than 10 per cent., the countries for which, by this standard, we know the number of births and deaths, comprise only about one-third of the population of the earth. One hundred years ago the proportion was only about one-twelfth.

Our knowledge of the numbers of inhabitants is more satisfactory. The countries which have taken censuses comprise perhaps three-quarters of the population of the earth. The most populous countries which so far have not taken censuses are: China, Afghanistan, Arabia, Iraq, Iran, Nepal, Syria; Ethiopia,

Liberia, Belgian Congo, Ruanda-Urundi, Kenya, Sudan, Mozambique; Ecuador. But the last census was taken in Argentine in 1914, in Uruguay in 1908, in Bolivia in 1900, in Paraguay in 1899, in Peru in 1876. In other countries, like French West Africa or Indo-China, the censuses are quite inadequate. If we include only those countries for which a census has been taken since 1921, or for which the published numbers can safely be said neither to exceed nor to lag behind the actual numbers of inhabitants by more than 10 per cent., the countries for which, by this standard, we know the population, comprise perhaps only three-fifths of the population of the earth. One hundred years ago the proportion was hardly one-fifth.

The *terra incognita* has thus been greatly reduced; but the number of countries for which we can study population trends is still small. It is small not only because in many countries collection of the pertinent statistics was begun rather recently; it is small also, paradoxically enough, because in many countries the data have become more accurate. The improvements in census technique and in birth and death registration are a particularly serious source of error because it is impossible, as a rule, numerically to appraise their purport. The official birth-rate of England was 32·3 in 1841–5 and 35·5 in 1871–5. No one doubts that birth registration had become more complete in the meantime. But no one can tell how much of the apparent increase was due to better registration. The official number of Maori births in 1934 was twice as high as in 1927.[1] It is evident that the New Zealand Government statistician was mistaken when, in publishing the 1927 figure, he stated that it 'may be regarded as normal'.[2] Birth registration until 1932 was quite deficient; but no one can tell from the official figures what was the actual trend of fertility. According to the census publications the population of French Equatorial Africa was 9,000,000 in 1911, 2,851,000 in 1921, and 3,130,000 in 1926.[3] The high figure of 9,000,000 in 1911 was evidently arrived at by over-estimating the population of territories where no actual census could be taken. But it also seems likely that the small figure of 2,851,000 for 1921 was due to omissions. It is evident that such figures do not tell anything about population trends.

Every student of population trends, therefore, should realize first of all that our knowledge of the number of inhabitants of the earth is rather vague.

[1] The number of registered Maori births in 1926–34 was: 1,536; 1,495; 1,845; 2,216; 2,124; 2,312; 2,745; 2,948; 2,981. See *New Zealand Official Year-Book*, 1932, p. 105, 1936, p. 82.

[2] See ibid., 1929, p. 128.

[3] See Statistique générale de la France, *Résultats statistiques du recensement général de la population*, 1911, vol. i, part i, p. 98; 1921, vol. i, part i, p. 115; 1926, vol. i, part i, p. 114.

If he reads, for instance, that the world's population is now 2,080 millions, he should accept such a statement with great reserve. My own computations lead me to the conclusion that the actual number lies somewhere between 1,880 and 2,260 millions.

Africa, fifteen years ago, was a dark continent for which all population estimates were more or less bold guesses. To-day the available statistical evidence for many sections is still quite defective, but it is safe to say that the total population is not less than 137 millions and not more than 165 millions. One hundred years ago the number of whites (of European descent) was negligible; it amounted to about 135,000.[1] To-day Africa has about 4 million whites.[2] Whether the natives have increased or decreased in number during the last 100 years is impossible to say.

For Asia the uncertainty to-day is larger than for Africa. The estimates for China alone vary between 325 and 525 millions. The present population of Asia may be as low as 960 millions, it may be as high as 1,260 millions. We know here, on the other hand, a little more about population trends. We know at least enough to be able to say that the total population has increased in the course of the last 100 years by over 300 millions.[3] But in view of the great un-

---

[1] See Appendix, Table I.　　　　[2] See Appendix, Table II.
[3] Walter F. Willcox (National Bureau of Economic Research, *International Migrations*, vol. ii, pp. 72–8, New York, 1931), on the

certainty as to the population trends of China, it is practically impossible to fix an upper limit. All that we can say is that the population very likely did not more than double in the last 100 years.

For South America the statistical evidence is now much poorer than it was fifteen years ago. But the data for North America are so trustworthy that the margin of error in estimating the population of the whole continent is smaller than for either Africa or Asia. It is safe to say that the population is not smaller than 250 millions and not larger than 280 millions. The whites now number between 168 and 178 millions, and the negroes between 36 and 42 millions.[1] A hundred years ago the whites numbered 18 or 20 millions and the negroes nearly 10 millions.[2] We know practically nothing of the number of Indians in former times and very little about their present numbers. But there cannot be any

best available evidence, estimated that the population of Asia, excluding China, has increased from 329 millions in 1850 to 612 millions in 1929, or by 283 millions. The League of Nations *Statistical Year-Book* gives for Asia, excluding China, 671·2 millions (31 Dec. 1933). Willcox assumes that the population of China in 1929 was the same as in 1850. Although I deem it quite likely that the population of China has not increased since 1910 I do not think that the same is true for 1850–1910 (see Kuczynski, 'Population', *Encyclopaedia of the Social Sciences*, vol. xii, p. 242, New York, 1934). But even if it were so, the total population of Asia would have increased by more than 300 millions since 1835.

[1] See Appendix, Table IV.   [2] See Appendix, Table III.

doubt that a hundred years ago the whites in America constituted only a minority of the population while at present they probably comprise nearly two-thirds.

For Oceania, the available data, on the whole, are quite satisfactory. It is safe to say that the population now is not less than 10 and not more than 11 millions. The persons of European descent number more than 8 millions[1] as against about 120,000 in 1835.[2] The natives are less numerous than a hundred years ago, but it is impossible to say by how much.

For Europe the population can be reckoned now at 522 or 542 millions. A hundred years ago it was about 240 millions. In 1770 it was only about 150 millions.

The two most outstanding facts of which we have some numerical knowledge, then, are: the peopling of America with whites and blacks, and the population growth of Europe.

ii. THE PEOPLING OF AMERICA WITH BLACKS

The peopling of America with whites and blacks began almost simultaneously. The number of negroes brought over from Spain was small at first, and in 1503 the Governor of Hispaniola (Haiti) even

[1] See Appendix, Table V.

[2] The total population of Australia (excluding aboriginals) is estimated at 113,354 for 31 December 1835 (see *Australian Demography*, Bulletin No. 45, p. 238). The European population on the other islands was very small.

asked to stop the sending of negroes, 'because they fled amongst the Indians and taught them bad customs and never could be captured'.[1] But there is evidence that negroes were dispatched again from 1505 on,[2] and a royal decree of 1511 provided that a large number be carried from Guinea to the new possessions 'since the labour of a negro was more useful than that of four Indians'.[3] Seven years later Charles V authorized a Flemish gentleman of his Court to import 4,000 negro slaves into Haiti, Porto Rico, Cuba, and Jamaica.[4] The supply of negroes to the Spanish colonies became from this time a regular branch of commerce. The number of negroes exported from Africa was greatly increased by the settlement of the Portuguese in Brazil.[5] About 1600 the Dutch began to ship slaves to America, and the French soon followed their example and sent huge numbers of negroes to their newly acquired colonies in the West Indies.

[1] See Antonio de Herrera, *Historia General de los Hechos de los Castellanos en las Islas i Tierra Firme del Mar Oceano*, vol. i, part i, p. 180, Madrid, 1601.

[2] See Georges Scelle, *La traite négrière aux Indes de Castille*, vol. i, p. 123, Paris, 1906.

[3] See Herrera, vol. i, part i, p. 297.

[4] The patent dated 18 August 1518 is printed in Scelle, vol. i, p. 755.

[5] According to a report submitted to the King of Portugal in 1592 (see extract published in Paiva Manso, *Historia do Congo*, pp. 137–41, Lisbon, 1877), 52,053 negro slaves were carried from Angola to Brazil between 1575 and 1591.

The first Englishman to engage in the African slave trade to America was John Hawkins in 1562. Being 'assured that Negroes were very good marchandise in Hispaniola, and that store of Negroes might easily be had upon the coast of Guinea', he went to Sierra Leone, 'and got into his possession, partly by the sword, and partly by other meanes, to the nomber of 300 Negroes at the least', whom he sold in Haiti.[1] But Hawkins's slave raids were a solitary instance.[2] The English, then, had no colonies to use negro labour, and when in the early seventeenth century they acquired such colonies in the West Indies and on the North American continent, they obtained their first, rather small, supplies from the slave traders of other European nations. But when, with the introduction of sugar-cane from Brazil to Barbados in 1641,[3] the English demand for negroes grew, they themselves began to import large numbers of slaves from Africa. This trade was increased considerably after the occupation of Jamaica in 1655. Soon the English began to supply also the Spanish colonies with slaves. At the beginning of the eighteenth century they brought more negroes to America

[1] See Richard Hakluyt, *The Principall Navigations, Voiages and Discoveries of the English Nation*, pp. 521–2, London, 1589.

[2] See James Bandinel, *Some Account of the Trade in Slaves from Africa*, p. 44, London, 1842.

[3] See A. Anderson, *Historical and Chronological Deduction of the Origin of Commerce*, vol. ii, p. 72, London, 1764.

than any other European nation with the exception perhaps of the Portuguese, and in the course of the following hundred years they imported at times more slaves than all the other European nations put together.

The abolition of the slave trade by Great Britain and other nations at the beginning of the nineteenth century greatly restricted the number of American countries into which negroes could be imported, but it did not reduce the yearly number of negroes imported into America. So great was the demand of Brazil and Cuba that in the second half of the 1830's more negroes were shipped from Africa to America than in any previous quinquennial period. From 1845 on, Brazil was the only American country to absorb large numbers of slaves[1] and this trade, too, became negligible after 1860.

What was the total number of slaves imported into America? Many attempts to answer this question have been made in the course of the last 150 years, but none of the answers is quite satisfactory since the underlying data are not conclusive. We know, for instance, that 676,276 negro slaves were legally imported into Jamaica from the time of the British conquest in 1655 to December 1787,[2] and we have

[1] See *Fourth Report from the Select Committee on the Slave Trade,* 1848, p. 3 (*Parliamentary Papers, 1847–8,* vol. 22, p. 707).

[2] According to the custom house records; see *Report of the Lords*

similar authentic figures for many other colonies for shorter periods. We know, for instance, that 47,146 negroes were carried in British vessels in 1771 from Africa to America,[1] and we have authoritative estimates of the numbers carried in other years by British and by other vessels. But since many slaves were re-exported from one colony to another,[2] since importations owing to wars and other reasons fluctuated very much, and since the estimates, especially for the importations into Brazil, are most conflicting, it is very risky to piece together the various data to be found in the official reports and the private publications of the various countries. The estimate of the total importations of negro slaves into America which on the whole seems to me the most acceptable reads as follows:[3]

16th century	.	.	. nearly	900,000
17th century	.	.	. .	2,750,000
18th century	.	.	. .	7,000,000
19th century	.	.	. over	4,000,000
		Total, perhaps		15,000,000

of the Committee of Council appointed for the Consideration of all Matters relating to Trade and Foreign Plantations 1789, part iii.

[1] See Bryan Edwards, *The History, Civil and Commercial, of the British West Indies*, 5th ed., vol. ii, p. 65, London, 1819.

[2] Of the 676,276 negroes imported in 1655–1787 into Jamaica, 160,446 were re-exported.

[3] See W. E. B. DuBois, 'The Negro Race in the United States of America', *Papers on Inter-racial Problems communicated to the First Universal Races Congress, London, 1911*, p. 349, London, 1911.

The total of 15 millions is rather a conservative estimate. It is unlikely that the actual number was smaller but it is quite possible that it was larger. On the other hand, the evidence available so far, it seems to me, does not permit the total to be put much higher. Exaggerations in this field are still common. The author of one of the best recent books on the slave trade states: 'The number of blacks exported to the West Indies from 1511 to 1789 is estimated at 40 or 50 millions.'[1] Another writer contends that from the second half of the seventeenth century until the abolition of slavery in 1889 'no fewer than 30 million blacks, according to the most moderate estimates of Brazilian historians, were shipped to Brazil'.[2]

In order, however, to avoid every misunderstanding, I want to point out that the total number of victims of the African slave trade was probably several times as high as the number of negroes imported into America, and this for the following reasons:

1. Negroes have been exported not only to America, but also to Asia and to Europe.[3] There was,

[1] P. Dieudonné Rinchon, *La traite et l'esclavage des Congolais par les Européens*, p. 96, Brussels, 1929.

[2] Benjamin Péret, 'Black and White in Brazil', in Nancy Cunard, *Negro Anthology*, p. 510, London, 1934.

[3] It is a well-known fact that negroes are still to-day exported from Africa to Asia. What is perhaps less well known is that from

moreover, a very active slave trade within the African continent, numerous negroes being brought to the Mediterranean countries or sold to the African colonies of the various European nations.

2. Many millions of negroes died either in raids and wars undertaken by African chieftains for the

the fifteenth till the eighteenth century considerable numbers of negro slaves were brought to Europe. I shall confine myself to giving a few data on the first century of negro slave trade to Portugal:

In 1453 Gomez Eannes de Azurara, in his *Chronica do Descobrimento e Conquista de Guiné* (p. 454, Paris, 1841), reported that 927 slaves were brought from Guinea to Portugal in 1441–8.

In 1455 the Venetian da Cadamosto, in the description of his voyage along the coast of Africa, relates: 'Every year between 700 and 800 slaves are sent from Argin to Portugal' (see Ramusio, *Primo Volume delle Navigationi et Viaggi*, p. 108, Venice, 1550).

In 1535 Nicolaus Clenardus writes from Evora that there is such a mass of slaves in Portugal that he could believe there are more slaves than free Portuguese (see his charming letter of 26 March 1535 to his instructor Jacobus Latomus in *Epistolarum Libri Duo*, p. 11, Antwerp, 1566).

In 1541 the historian Damianus a Goes states that 10,000 or 12,000 slaves a year are brought to Portugal from the kingdom of Nigritia, apart from others brought from Mauretania, India, and Brazil (see 'Hispania', a treatise dated Louvain, 12 December 1541, in *Aliquot Opuscula*, Louvain, 1544).

Negro slaves were likewise imported from Africa into Spain and Italy. As for England, there were no direct imports from Africa, but African slaves were brought by their masters from the colonies in America. In 1772 there were thus in England 14,000 or 15,000 negro slaves (see T. B. Howell, *A Complete Collection of State Trials*, 'The Case of James Sommersett, a Negro, on a Habeas Corpus, King's-Bench 1771–72', vol. xx, cols. 72, 77, 79, London, 1814).

sole purpose of supplying the foreign demand for slaves, or after their seizure on the march from the interior to the coast, or in the slave yards waiting for embarkation, or on board the ships to America.[1]

Until the abolition of the slave trade the peopling of America with blacks was carried on with terrible waste. But conditions were by no means uniform. The number of slaves imported into the United States probably did not exceed 500,000; their natural increase was so large that, at the date of the abolition of the trade, negroes in the United States numbered nearly 1,300,000. The number of slaves imported into Jamaica and not re-exported was about 700,000;[2] at the date of the abolition of the trade, negroes in Jamaica numbered about 350,000. The supplies necessary to replenish and increase the stocks of slaves were much larger still, for example, in the French West Indian colonies. The divergencies were due to differences in the rates of mortality and of procreation. Mortality, practically everywhere, was high until the abolition of slavery.

[1] See Thomas Fowell Buxton, *The African Slave Trade*, London, 1839; Gaston-Martin, *L'ère des négriers*, Paris, 1931. It may be mentioned incidentally that an all-inclusive computation of the victims of the slave trade should also comprise, for instance, the hundreds of thousands of European sailors who prematurely died as crews of slave ships.

[2] 1655–1787: 510,000; 1788–99: 118,000 (see H. C. Carey, *The Slave Trade*, pp. 9–10, London, 1853); 1799–1807: 79,000 (see *Brief Remarks on the Slave Registry Bill*, p. 68, London, 1816).

As early as 1511 the Spanish king wrote to an official in the West Indies: 'I do not understand how so many negroes have died; take much care of them.'[1] Where mortality was excessive it was mainly due to diseases or reckless exploitation. Low fertility of female slaves has been attributed chiefly to excessive fatigue, to privations, to premature and promiscuous intercourse, to venereal diseases, and to deliberate abortions.[2] But low fertility was probably not the main reason for keeping the rate of procreation low in most colonies. The decisive factor, as I see it, was the disproportion in the number of males and females. If the proportion of negresses among the slaves imported into the United States had been as small as into the West Indies, which for their sugar plantations required mainly male labourers, the prevailing fertility and mortality would perhaps not have resulted in any excess of births over deaths.

Since the abolition of the slave trade the reproduction of the negro population has been intensified considerably in America as a whole. The effect was small in the United States where reproduction had been large before the abolition of the trade; in some countries, on the other hand, reproduction remained low after the abolition of the trade and began to

[1] See Arthur Helps, *The Spanish Conquest in America*, new ed., vol. i, p. 173, London and New York, 1900.
[2] See, for instance, *Report 1789*, part iii.

increase only after the abolition of slavery. In a crude manner the changes in the peopling of America with blacks may be indicated as follows: until 1836 at least 12 million negroes were imported into America resulting in a total negro population of nearly 10 millions. In the last one hundred years 2 million negroes at the utmost were brought to America, but the total negro population increased from nearly 10 millions to nearly 40 millions.

iii. The Peopling of America with Whites

For a very long period the peopling of America with whites encountered even greater difficulties than the peopling of America with blacks. Mortality among the whites was higher still than among the negro slaves. The proportion of females among the whites was lower still than among the negroes. Moreover, many disappointed white emigrants returned to Europe.

On his first trip in 1492 Columbus sailed with 90 men. He left in America about 40, who all perished within a year. On his second trip in 1493 he sailed with 1,500 men, and quite a few more Spanish vessels went to Haiti before Ovando, in 1502, arrived with his large expedition of 2,500 men. But the population remained small. Of the 2,500 men brought across by Ovando over 1,000 died of disease shortly after their arrival, and of all those who had come there in previous years not more than 300 were then still living on the island.[1] And yet mortality was by no means exceptionally high among these early Spanish colonists. It was much higher, for example, among the English settlers in Virginia in the early seventeenth century.

I do not know of any estimate of the total number of immigrants to America prior to the nineteenth century, and most estimates made for single countries inspire little confidence. Rosseeuw St.-Hilaire, in his monumental history of Spain, says that nearly 3 million Spaniards emigrated to the New World in the first 150 years after its discovery,[2] and that hardly any returned.[3] Since he states that the total number of Spaniards settled in the colonies sixty years after the conquest did not exceed 15,000,[4] emigration on a large scale cannot have started before 1550, and St.-Hilaire must have assumed that emigration in the following ninety years averaged about 30,000. But quite apart from other considerations it seems altogether unlikely that Spain at that time had enough ocean ships to carry so many emigrants with the necessary supplies to America. When Columbus prepared for his second voyage, which he undertook with 17 ships and 1,500 men, the owners of all vessels

---

[1] See Herrera, vol. i, part i, pp. 19, 54, 61, 156, 161.
[2] See *Histoire d'Espagne*, new ed., vol. x, p. 354, Paris, 1869.
[3] See, for instance, vol. xiii, p. 29, Paris, 1878.
[4] See ibid., vol. xiii, p. 22.

throughout the ports of Andalusia were required by
a royal ordinance to hold them in readiness for the
expedition,[1] and there is no evidence that the
Spanish merchant marine at the end of the sixteenth
century was larger than at the end of the fifteenth
century. But St.-Hilaire is by no means the only
authority who has over-estimated the extent of
Spanish emigration to America.[2] Immigration into
British North America, on the other hand, is
generally under-estimated by gratifying the senti-
mental theory that the enormous increase of the
white population in the United States from 250,000
in 1700 to 4,300,000 in 1800 was almost solely due to
procreation on the part of the old sturdy stock.

That for former centuries much fewer accurate
data have been compiled on the immigration of the
whites than on the importation of negroes is mainly
due to the fact that a great deal of research work was
undertaken in connexion with the fight for the abolition of slavery, while there never has been a similar
incentive for the study of white immigration. This
is an explanation but not an excuse. The student of
white immigration, it is true, cannot avail himself of

[1] See William H. Prescott, *History of the Reign of Ferdinand and Isabella*, vol. ii, p. 256, London, 1838.

[2] According to René Gonnard (*Essai sur l'histoire de l'émigration*, pp. 96–7, Paris, 1928), the Spanish minister Campillo in 1742 estimated the yearly average number of Spanish emigrants to America
since 1492 at 14,000.

such material as is contained in the records of slave carrying companies or of customs authorities which collected duties on the importation of negroes; but he will find in the official reports and in the private publications of the countries of emigration and immigration a vast mass of material which, if carefully and critically pieced together, would enable him to enlarge greatly our numerical knowledge of white immigration to America in the pre-statistical period.[1] I can say this with a certain degree of assurance as I have myself made various attempts in this direction, all of which ended prematurely owing to interference of other work, which again is an explanation but not an excuse. As matters stand it is still impossible to estimate the number of white immigrants into America for former centuries. But it is safe to say that the total number of whites who until 1820 immigrated and did not return was at least 3 millions. I should not wonder if a thorough investigation would lead to a much higher figure.

From about 1820 on we are on more solid ground, since we have, for an ever-increasing number of

---

[1] The result would be much more satisfactory still if a systematic attempt were made to explore the archives of the various countries. The archives of Sevilla, for instance, contain an enormous number of not yet utilized lists of colonial emigrant permits dating as far back as 1509 and coming down to 1834, some of them arranged according to countries of destination (see *International Migrations*, vol. i, p. 61).

European and American countries, statistics bearing on overseas emigration and immigration. But it would be a mistake to assume that it ought to be an easy task to derive from these statistics the total number of European immigrants to America for the last 115 years. I must confine myself to mentioning a few reasons:

1. The statistics of many countries do not cover the entire period; those of Mexico start with the year 1909.

2. The statistics of all countries are more or less incomplete; the immigration statistics of the United States until 1864 were based on passenger lists which, in part, were very defective; even the most careful immigration statistics cannot include, for instance, deserting sailors.

3. The statistics in many cases do not include emigrants and immigrants only; the statistics of the United States until 1 January 1868 and of Great Britain until 1 April 1912 comprised all passengers.

Taking account of the defects in the statistics, I estimate the total number of European immigrants to America from 1820 to 1935 at about 55 millions.[1]

[1] According to a compilation by Ferenczi (see *International Migrations*, vol. i, p. 168), the total number of overseas immigrants to America from 1821 to 1924 was 50,307,500. This figure includes immigrants from other continents than Europe and also a large number of passengers who did not intend to reside in America. It comprises, on the other hand, only those American countries for which statistics were available, the number of countries included varying between 2 and 12, and it does not make allowance for omissions in the official statistics.

But a large proportion of these immigrants have returned to Europe. I estimate the total number of European immigrants who stayed in America for the rest of their lives at about 35 millions.

The total number of permanent white immigrants into America since 1492 may thus have been nearly 40 millions as against an importation of at least 15 million negroes. Since the total number of whites in America is at present about 172 millions, as against nearly 40 million negroes, reproduction of the whites was much greater.

The overseas emigration from Europe to other continents was much less important. Until 1836 hardly more than 40,000 emigrants could have gone to Australia, apart from 103,000 convicts deported to New South Wales and Tasmania.[1] The total number of permanent European immigrants to Australia and New Zealand (including deported criminals) has been, up till now, about 2,800,000. The total net immigration of Europeans into Africa was probably smaller.[2]

Of the net overseas emigration of Europeans since 1492, amounting to about 45 millions, something like 24 millions went to the United States, 15 millions to other countries of America, and 6 millions to other continents.

[1] See *International Migrations*, vol. i, p. 102.
[2] Permanent overseas migration to Asia has been very slight (continental migration from European to Asiatic Russia does not concern us here).

II

i. Reduction of Mortality

PRIOR to the eighteenth century there was apparently no definite population trend in Europe as a whole. We have no reason to assume that the population in 1700 was any larger than in 1600, or that the population in 1600 was much larger than in 1300. There is no doubt that the population increased considerably between 1700 and 1770. But we do not know how large this increase was. Since 1770 the population has increased by about 250 per cent.; it is now $3\frac{1}{2}$ times as large as 165 years ago.

This enormous increase occurred in spite of a very large emigration. In 1770 only about 4 million persons of European stock lived in other continents. To-day there are in America alone about 172 million persons of European stock, not counting some dozens of millions of mulattos and mestizos with partly European blood. The total number of persons of European stock in the world is now about 720 millions as against about 155 millions in 1770. Their average yearly increase was nearly one per cent.

What it means that the white population in the last 165 years increased by nearly one per cent. per year can perhaps best be understood if one realizes that if such a rate of increase had prevailed in England since Caesar's invasion, one couple living at that time would by now have 720 million descendants. One may also put it like this: if the white population had increased since 1300 as it has increased since 1770 it would now number something like 40,000 millions; the whole world would then be settled as densely by whites as England is now.

Prior to the eighteenth century, therefore, there cannot have been a definite population trend. Periods having an excess of births must have alternated with periods having an excess of deaths. What took place, as a rule, was that in so-called normal years births exceeded deaths, while in periods of famines and especially of epidemics deaths exceeded births. Similar conditions still prevail, for example, in Africa and in China. But in Europe, since 1770, births have exceeded deaths in probably every single year except 1916, 1917, and 1918.

This striking change in the population trend of Europe, and in general of countries predominantly inhabited by whites, is usually explained by the coincidence of a decrease of mortality and an increase of natality. But there is no conclusive proof of an increase of natality. Natality was certainly not constant. The available statistics indicate ups and downs all through the period from 1750 to 1885, but they reveal no marked trend in either direction. The enormous growth of the white population, it seems to me, is due exclusively to a decrease of mortality.

Mortality was reduced mainly through progress achieved in the field of (preventive) hygiene and (curative) medicine. Without such progress the white population, at least in Europe, would possibly have remained stationary as it did in many former centuries. But hygienic and medical progress alone did not render possible the actual excess of births over deaths. Such progress, it is true, would in any case have reduced mortality from certain diseases; but famines, economic wars, or birth-control would have largely prevented the ensuing population increase if hygienic and medical progress had not been accompanied by an economic and technical revolution which enormously enlarged the available means of subsistence for those living in Europe, and at the same time made possible the emigration of dozens of millions of Europeans to the United States and other overseas countries.

The reduction of mortality was very large but not quite as large as is usually believed. The most common method of measuring mortality consists in computing the crude death-rate, i.e. the yearly number of deaths per 1,000 inhabitants. This rate is calculated without regard to the age-composition of the population and, therefore, affords an adequate gauge of the trend of mortality only if the age-composition of the population does not change. But the age-composition in Europe has changed very much in the course of the last hundred years, and it so happens that the proportion of persons at ages where death claims most victims is now comparatively small. The crude death-rate, therefore, is now unduly low and exaggerates the reduction of mortality which can be measured adequately only through life-tables which eliminate all the misleading effects of the actual age-composition. I may mention as an illustration that the crude death-rate of England has decreased in the last ninety years by nearly one-half, while the correct death-rate derived from the life-table has decreased by one-third.

The first life-table of any country was computed in Sweden for 1755-75. It revealed a mean expectation of life at birth of 35 years. The expectation of life was probably shorter in most other countries of Europe. In the 1840's it was 46 years in Norway, 44 years in Sweden, 42 years in Denmark, 41 years in England, 40 years in France, and it was shorter still in many other European countries. In the 1890's it was 58 years in New Zealand, 53 years in Australia, 52 years in Sweden and Norway, 50 years in Denmark, 48 years in Holland, 47 years in Belgium and Switzerland, 46 years in England and Scotland, 44 years in Finland, 42 years in Germany, 37 years in Austria, and 33 years in Russia. In no country did the mean expectation of life reach 60 years before the twentieth century. It now exceeds 60 years, for example, in Denmark, Norway, and Sweden, in England, Germany, Holland, Switzerland, in the United States, in Australia, and New Zealand. In 1933 it was 61 years in England and 68 years in New Zealand. Forty years ago the mean expectation of life varied for the countries of Western civilization between about 37 and 58 years; it now varies only between about 57 and 68 years. This seems to indicate that progress has been particularly great where improvement started late or was at first slow. It is even possible that if we had early life-tables for all countries, we might find that the total relative improvement in most countries predominantly inhabited by whites has been pretty much the same since 1770. For these countries as a whole the expectation of life has nearly doubled, and this is the explanation for the stupendous growth of the white population in the last 165 years from about 155 millions to about 720 millions.

But this decrease of mortality was by no means equally distributed over all age groups. It was in most countries largest for infants, i.e. children under one year. Infant mortality is usually computed by relating the number of deaths under one year to the number of births of the same calendar year. What is the range of infant mortality by this standard? In former times rates exceeding 300 per 1,000 were nothing unusual. Such rates prevailed until sixty years ago in southern Germany, and the rate for Chile in 1933 and 1934 was still 260. The rate for Sweden has declined from 200 in the second half of the eighteenth century to 100 at the end of the nineteenth century and to 50 in 1933. It is still above 120 in some countries of central and eastern Europe such as Czechoslovakia, Hungary, Lithuania, Poland, the Balkan States, and also in Portugal. The lowest rate ever recorded was that of 31 in New Zealand for 1932 (excluding Maoris).

In England, infant mortality from 1838 to 1904 oscillated between 130 and 164, without showing any particular trend. In 1905 it dropped for the first time below 130. Since 1915 it has never reached 100. Since 1921 it has been below 80 all the time. In 1935 it was 57.

Mortality has also decreased considerably for children from 1 to 5 years. While 90 years ago only 74 out of 100 newly born survived the age of 5 in England, the percentage of survivors in 1933 was 91. At the age of 60, the percentages of survivors were 37 and 67 respectively. But the mean expectation of life of those 60 years old has only increased from 13·9 to 15·4 years. It is certainly a strange fact that while now two-thirds of the newly born reach the age of 60, as against only three-eighths 90 years ago, those who reach 60 now have only about the same expectation of life as those reaching 60 a century ago. Two explanations have been given for this phenomenon, which is to be found also in many other countries. There are people who say that those who reach 60 now are weaker, on an average, than a century ago because in former times only strong people reached the age of 60. But even granted that in former times only the fittest survived, they must themselves have undergone so much hardship in the first 60 years of their life that they were no longer strong afterwards. I, therefore, am inclined to accept the other explanation according to which, notwithstanding all progress in hygiene and medicine, mankind nowadays is just as unable to extend the life of old people as a century ago. If, then, we are to assume that the mean expectation of life of those who reach 60 will never reach 20 years, the expectation of life of the newly born could never reach 80 years, even if all the newly born survived the age of 60.

Before the reduction of mortality which began in the eighteenth century the mean expectation of life in Europe was probably something like 30 years. By the end of the nineteenth century it had increased in the territory covered by Western civilization to about 45 years. At present it is about 60 years. Even allowing for all conceivable advances in hygiene and medicine, it seems unlikely that it ever will increase by another 15 years. Mortality was the decisive factor in determining population growth in the past. The future population trend will depend mainly on fertility.

ii. REDUCTION OF FERTILITY

Fertility is a field in which many otherwise intelligent persons who are accustomed to judge by facts and figures adhere to certain preconceived ideas without ever taking the trouble of examining whether their argument is reconcilable with reality or not. This argument runs about as follows:

Up to the seventies or eighties of the last century most wives in civilized as well as uncivilized countries had very many children. This is still true, for instance, of southern and eastern Europe and likewise of the coloured races. Even in western Europe (with the exception of France) families with numerous children still constitute the rule in the rural districts and in the slums of the cities. But, on the whole, child-bearing capacity has decreased somewhat in the countries of Western civilization, and birth-control, which began about fifty years ago among the well-to-do and the educated, has become familiar to a considerable part of the urban middle class and has gained ground even beyond it. However, owing to the large reduction of mortality, the population even of western Europe is still mounting and, of course, will go on increasing at the same rate if fertility and mortality remain what they are. Moreover, mortality may be reduced still further, and population growth in any case is likely to be accelerated again as soon as a general improvement of economic conditions has eliminated the main motive for birth-control. Over-population which harasses most countries to-day, therefore, will become more and more disastrous.

How did the myth arise that in former times most families had very many children? Are the anthropologists and demographers by any chance to be blamed for it? This is certainly not the case. For uncivilized tribes anthropologists have reported probably as often a scarcity of children as an abundance of children. And as for Europe there was a consensus of opinion among demographers—from John Graunt, the founder of vital statistics (1662), on all through the eighteenth century and a considerable part of the nineteenth—that there were on an average four births per marriage. If, nevertheless, so many people to-day greatly over-estimate the former fertility in our countries and the former and the present fertility of many other nations, the causes seem to be firstly, an erroneous conception, and secondly, an optical illusion. The misconception is: birth-control is a recent western European invention; without birth-control most wives would inevitably bear many children. The optical illusion is that large families of the past appear to the uncritical observer of to-day more numerous than they actually were. The origin of this optical illusion can perhaps best be illustrated by an example: let us assume five married sisters who had 12, 6, 4, 2, and o children. Although only one of the five sisters had more than 6 children, one-half of the 24 children would rightly say that their mother had 12 children. Although one of the five sisters had no child, none of the 24 children would say that their mother was childless. The last fact is so obvious that it may seem ridiculous to mention it. And yet very few of the many people who point to the number of children of their grandmothers and mothers as proof of the high fertility of wives in former times *do* realize that grandmothers and mothers constitute a selected group which does not comprise a single woman who had no child. For fairness' sake it should be noted, by the way, that even eminent scholars have fallen victims of such an optical illusion. When Professor Winkler of the University of Vienna, in his recently published excellent text-book on statistics, speaks of an 'issue of 12 to 16 children, such as it was customary with our fathers',[1] he evidently did not realize that even if the majority of his generation could pride itself on having had fathers with 12 to 16 children, this would tell us nothing about the

[1] Wilhelm Winkler, *Grundriss der Statistik*, vol. ii, p. 104, Berlin, 1933.

frequency of such prolific fathers. And if over and over again scholars draw far-reaching conclusions from the incontrovertible fact that very many famous men are descendants of prolific parents, they evidently do not realize that they could have established the same fact for any other group of men. Children of prolific parents are more numerous than children of parents with few offspring; if one-half of all fathers had 10 children and the other half had 1 child, there would be 10 times as many children of prolific parents as of parents with few offspring. (I might also perhaps mention in this connexion one other factor which, with many people, may strengthen the illusion that most women in former times had many children: a man is more apt to remember relatives who had numerous descendants; he will think, for instance, more frequently of those uncles and aunts who provided him with cousins and left many grand-children than of those who died childless before he was born.)

If, however, we leave the field of personal impressions and consult the available statistics we shall find that in western, northern, and southern Europe the average fertility in former times was actually much lower than most people imagine. Wives with 8 or more children constituted a small minority and wives who had more than 5 children were probably not more numerous than those who had less. Fertility was higher in eastern Europe and also, for example, in

French Canada. For most of the coloured races the available statistics are too scanty to permit a final judgement. It is possible that fertility in China was, and still is, as high as it used to be in eastern Europe, and the same may be true of some other Asiatic, South American, and Central American countries; but, according to the statistics of Japan, fertility neither in the past nor at present exceeds there the level formerly maintained in western, northern, and southern Europe. It is possible that in former times fertility among the negroes in the United States was as high as in eastern Europe, but it is now exceedingly low. Many uncivilized nations seem never to have been very fertile; others apparently have lost their fertility for good through contact with the whites; others still (like the Maoris) have recuperated their former strong fertility, after having lost it temporarily through contact with the whites.

What is theoretically the range of fertility? The upper limit of fertility (actual production of children) is determined by fecundity (child-bearing capacity); it would be reached if all females gave birth to as many children as they possibly could. The lower limit is zero; it would be reached in a 100 per cent. successful general birth strike.

Fecundity, the upper limit of fertility, has not been always and everywhere the same. The question whether it has increased or decreased with progressing civilization is a controversial one. Malthus and Darwin, for example, were of the opinion that the reproductive power is less in barbarous than in civilized races. Carr-Saunders, to mention only one recent demographer, holds the same view. Darwin considers it 'highly probable that savages, who often suffer much hardship, and who do not obtain so much nutritious food as civilised men, would be actually less prolific'.[1] Herbert Spencer, on the other hand, was of the opinion that, other things being equal, advancing evolution must be accompanied by declining fecundity, and that, in the highest types, fecundity must still further decrease if evolution still further increases.[2] But he himself adds that though, other things being equal, the civilized would be less prolific than the savages, 'yet, other things are so unequal, as to make it quite conformable to the general law that they should be more prolific'.[3] The main inequality, according to him, consists in the amount and quality of food.

An increase of the reproductive power through an improvement in living conditions, especially through a more regular and more rational food consumption, is conceivable in two ways. It is possible that the child-bearing period be expanded, or that the child-

---

[1] Charles Darwin, *The Descent of Man*, vol. i, p. 132, London, 1871.
[2] See Herbert Spencer, *The Principles of Biology*, vol. ii, p. 411, London, 1867.   [3] Ibid., p. 489.

bearing capacity be intensified. Carr-Saunders emphasizes the first possibility:

'Good conditions also influence the age at which menstruation begins. The better the conditions, the earlier does it begin. Further, it is also known that the mature period tends to be prolonged where conditions are good. It is known, for example, that the mature period comes to an end earlier among the labouring than among the richer classes. Therefore good conditions tend to be connected not only with an earlier beginning but also with a longer duration of the mature period.'[1]

I am inclined to lay more stress on the second possibility, the intensification of child-bearing capacity. Statistical evidence shows an enormous decrease of fertility in times of famine. In Finland the number of births thus fell from 59,164 in 1867 to 43,757 in 1868.[2] In the five largest cities of the Ukraine the birth-rate in 1922 was as low as 15; it rose from 15 in the last quarter of that year to 22 in the first quarter of 1923 and to 32 in the second quarter, and it remained at about that level until 1926.[3] It is true that in such chaotic times the decrease in the number of marriages and the disruption of families somewhat

[1] A. M. Carr-Saunders, *The Population Problem, A Study in Human Evolution*, p. 92, Oxford, 1922.

[2] See *Éléments démographiques principaux de la Finlande 1750–1890*, vol. ii, p. 149, Helsingfors, 1902.

[3] See Kuczynski, *The Balance of Births and Deaths*, vol. ii, p. 17, Washington, 1931.

affect fertility. As a matter of fact legitimate births decreased in Finland from 1867 to 1868 by 26 per cent., while illegitimate births decreased by 21 per cent.[1] But is not this decrease of illegitimate births by as much as 21 per cent. a conclusive proof of a decrease of fecundity, i.e. of child-bearing capacity?

Don't be daft.

Famines now occur less frequently than in former times but they are, of course, not the only factor affecting fecundity. You will find in the literature of the subject an immense catalogue of such factors; for example, premature or too frequent cohabitation, venereal and other diseases, deliberate abortions, extended lactation, intemperance in feeding and drinking, physical or mental overwork. But with some of these factors it is doubtful whether they are more prevalent now than in former times; with others it is doubtful whether they have ever been numerically important. Moreover, prejudices in this field play a large role. Marriages of girls under 16 are now generally considered as detrimental. They may be so in many respects. But do they actually affect child-bearing capacity? Marriages of girls under 16 seem to have been quite common in Europe in the seventeenth and eighteenth centuries. Louis XIV imposed a fine upon the fathers in French Canada who did not marry their daughters when they were

[1] See *Éléments démographiques*, vol. ii, pp. 129, 139.

16.[1] And there is ample evidence of French Canadian women who had their first child at 14 or 15 years and had 20 or more children thereafter.

The question whether fecundity has increased or decreased with progressing civilization is a controversial one. I am inclined rather to think that it has increased. But so far as the whites are concerned, the change in fecundity in the last centuries, whether it was an increase or not, must have been very small, and we may therefore assume that for them the upper limit of fertility was on the whole practically constant.

This upper limit would be reached only if all females, throughout their entire child-bearing period, had intercourse with procreative men and did nothing to prevent conception or to procure abortion. Since these conditions are never and nowhere fulfilled, fertility always and everywhere lags behind fecundity. But the degree to which fertility lags behind fecundity varies, of course, a great deal.

In England, till a few decades ago, abstinence of unmarried females was generally considered the most decisive factor in keeping fertility below fecundity. There were, to be sure, as early as the seventeenth century, writers who, in discussing population growth, pointed to practices preventing conception and pro-

[1] See Kuczynski, *Birth Registration and Birth Statistics in Canada*, p. 35, Washington, 1930.

curing abortion, and also to differential fertility between urban and rural dwellers, between the well-to-do and the poor. But they referred merely to birth-control on the part of unmarried women, and they did not intimate that differential fertility of married women was due to any deliberate action, but rather to impotence of the husband, barrenness of the wife, the abuse of spirituous liquors, and luxurious and unwholesome manner of living.[1]

In France, birth-control by married women as a demographically important factor was discussed apparently for the first time in 1778 by Moheau:

'Consult those men whom religion has established as trustees of the secret of the hearts and the weaknesses of humanity, or those whom a taste for factual investigations of importance for the welfare of the State has made accurate observers of the ways of country people and of the poor; they will tell you that the wealthy women for whom pleasure constitutes the greatest concern and the sole occupation are not the only ones to look upon the propagation of the species as an imposition belonging to bygone times (*une duperie du vieux temps*). Even now these baneful secrets, unknown to every animal other than man, have permeated to the countryside; nature sees itself cheated in the very villages.

'If these licentious practices, if these homicidal tastes spread further, they will not be less fatal to the State than the plagues which devastated it formerly; it is high time to

[1] See Kuczynski, 'British Demographers' Opinions on Fertility, 1660–1760', *Annals of Eugenics*, vol. vi, part ii, June 1935.

put a stop to this secret and terrible cause of depopulation which imperceptibly saps the nation and to which a short time hence we may attend too late.'[1]

The trend of fertility in France shows that the complaints of Moheau and others did not check the spread of birth-control. It gained more and more ground and, towards the middle of the nineteenth century, was probably practised by the majority of French families. But this is not true of other European countries. Birth-control by married women was probably more frequent in England in 1850 than in 1750, but fertility of marriages as a whole did not decline before the 1880's. There is, as a matter of fact, no evidence for any other European country but

[1] Moheau, *Recherches et considérations sur la population de la France*, part ii, pp. 101–2, Paris, 1778. That birth-control by married women had not been a long-time habit in France may also perhaps be inferred from the fact that Messance, who in 1766 (see *Recherches sur la population d'Auvergne*, &c., p. 143) considered it physically impossible that tax exemptions granted to fathers of numerous children could lead to an increase of births ('the fertility of the marriages depends on causes absolutely independent of the wish even of those who can alone contribute to it, and is for this reason above all laws made by men'), in 1788 (*Nouvelles recherches sur la population de la France*, p. 27) mentioned among the effects of the depravation of morals upon the population:

'The reasoning which induces man to wish for only one or two children.

'That style of false grandeur which induces man to have a large number of servants, a large number of guests at his table instead of seeing himself surrounded by his children; and worst of all, that greatest depravation of destroying in the very act of sowing.'

France that fertility in marriage was lower in the 1870's than in former times.

In the last fifty years the decrease has been enormous in nearly all countries predominantly inhabited by whites; it has been greater even than is usually believed. The most common method of measuring fertility consists in computing the crude birth-rate, i.e. the yearly number of births per 1,000 inhabitants. This rate is calculated without regard to the age-composition of the population and therefore affords an adequate gauge of the trend of fertility only if the age-composition of the population and, in particular, the proportion of women at child-bearing age does not change. But this proportion has increased considerably in most countries. The crude birth-rate, therefore, is now unduly high and makes the decrease of fertility appear smaller than it actually has been. The best method of measuring the decrease of fertility consists in computing the gross reproduction rate, which shows the average number of girls born to a woman who lives through child-bearing age.[1]

Fifty years ago the gross reproduction rate for western and northern Europe as a whole was 2·1. This means that about 210 girls (and about 220 boys) were born to 100 (married or unmarried) women passing through child-bearing age. By 1911–14 the

[1] For details see Kuczynski, *The Measurement of Population Growth*, pp. 106–30, London, 1935.

gross reproduction rate had fallen to 1·6. It dropped below unity in 1931 and was 0·9 in 1933. This means that according to fertility for 1933 not more than 90 girls were born to 100 women passing through child-bearing age.

Conditions, of course, are not uniform all over western and northern Europe, and the differences are still more marked if one compares the fertility of all countries predominantly inhabited by whites. The gross reproduction rate has been below 1 in England and Austria since 1926, in Germany and Sweden since 1928, in Norway since 1931, in Estonia since 1932, in France and Latvia since 1933. It is probably still slightly above 1 in Denmark, Czecho-slovakia, Hungary, Finland, the United States, Australia, and New Zealand. But it is now lower in each of these countries than it was in England and Sweden until 1925. It is nearly 1·4 in Canada, nearly 1·5 in Italy, about 1·6 in Poland and Lithuania, and about 1·8 in Bulgaria. In Bulgaria it is still about twice as high as in England, but even there is now lower than it was in most countries of western and northern Europe at the beginning of this century.

With the exception of Russia, where fertility, while being lower than before the World War, seems to be still at least as high as it was in western and northern Europe fifty years ago, practically all countries inhabited by whites have by now passed the stage through which western and northern Europe went in the 1880's and 1890's. The decrease of fertility began in some countries only after the World War, but where it started particularly late it was, as a rule, particularly rapid. This may indicate that where birth-control spread only recently the process was particularly rapid. One country, Germany, where fertility since the 1880's had decreased more than in any other country of the world—she had until 30 years ago the highest gross reproduction rate in western and northern Europe and in 1933 had the lowest—witnessed a marked increase in the number of births in 1934 and in the first half of 1935. But the figures published so far for the second half of 1935 indicate rather a downward trend, and in 1934 the gross reproduction rate was still below 1. With the fertility of 1934, the population of Germany and the population of western and northern Europe as a whole are doomed to die out even if every newly born girl reached the age of 50.

iii. The Balance of Births and Deaths

The usual method of establishing a balance of births and deaths consists in deducting the death-rate from the birth-rate. But this computation does not take account of the age-composition, and if the age-composition, as is the case, for example, in western

43

and northern Europe, tends to swell the birth-rate and to reduce the death-rate, the error is bound to be cumulative. The best method of establishing the balance of births and deaths consists in computing the net reproduction rate which shows (on the basis of present fertility and mortality) the average number of girls born to a newly born girl, or, what amounts to the same, the average number of future mothers born to a mother of to-day. The net reproduction rate, of course, must always be smaller than the gross reproduction rate. Both rates could only be equal if all newly born girls reached child-bearing age and passed through child-bearing age.

Fifty years ago the net reproduction rate in Germany, Denmark, and Sweden was 1·4 or 1·5. This means a doubling of the population within two generations. Conditions were more or less the same in the other countries of western and northern Europe with the exception of France and Ireland, where the net reproduction rate was about 1; the population there merely held its own. At present the rate is below 1 in all countries of western and northern Europe with the exception perhaps of Holland; it is likewise below 1 in Austria, Czechoslovakia, Hungary, Finland, Estonia, Latvia, the United States, Australia, and New Zealand. In western and northern Europe it has dropped from 1·3 in the 1880's to about 0·76 in 1933. This enormous fall in the net reproduction rate shows that fertility has decreased much more than mortality. The rate of 0·76 itself means that, according to fertility and mortality for 1933, 100 mothers give birth to only about 76 future mothers.

Let us look a little more closely at conditions in England. Since, at present, the proportion of children and of old persons is comparatively small, the number of births must be comparatively high. But the women who are now in child-bearing age will by and by pass this stage and will have to be fully replaced, if with present fertility the number of births is not to decrease. The chances of such a replacement in the near future are easy to ascertain. In 1934 there were in England 4,710,100 females under 15 years and 4,998,400 females from 15 to 30 years. It is evident that even if all girls who are now under 15 years reached child-bearing age, they would not be able to replace those who are now between 15 and 30 years.

The situation with which we are confronted can perhaps still better be realized by starting from the present number of female births. The total number of female births in 1934 was 290,768. The total number of women from 15 to 50 years was 11,109,200. If the yearly number of female births continued to be 290,768 and if no deaths occurred, in fifty years from now there would be 35 × 290,768, i.e. 10,176,880

45

women between 15 and 50 years, or 932,320 less than at present. But, according to present mortality, the average number of years which the newly born girls may expect to live in the age of child-bearing is 30. If, then, the number of female births continues to be 290,768, and if mortality under 50 remains constant, the number of women between 15 and 50 years, 50 years from now, would be $30 \times 290,768$, i.e. 8,723,040 only, as compared with 11,109,200 in 1934. But with present fertility the number of births is bound to decrease before then, since the number of women now between 15 and 30 years cannot be replaced by those now under 15 years of age.

What, then, will be the trend of the population? If fertility and mortality remain what they are, the population of England will still increase for some time to come. But the increase will become smaller and smaller, and deaths will exceed births long before the age-composition of the population will correspond to present fertility and mortality. Once the latter stage is reached, that is, roughly speaking, when there will be few women of child-bearing age because mothers have now few children, and when there will be many old people because mortality under 60 years has been so much reduced, the population, with a net reproduction rate of about 0·75, will decrease by about 25 per cent. within a generation, that is within about 30 years. Once the age-composition corresponding to present fertility and mortality is reached the population will thus amount

After 30 years to 75 per cent.
   „   60   „   56 „ „
   „   90   „   42 „ „
   „   120   „   32 „ „   &c.

The process may be accelerated by emigration, while it will not be affected by immigration since we are concerned only with the present population and its descendants. (Depopulation, of course, may be prevented by immigration.)

But the age-composition corresponding approximately to present fertility and mortality will not be reached before 1980, and it is of special interest to ascertain what would be the trend of the population in England in the next few decades. According to a computation carried out by Dr. Enid Charles, on the assumption that fertility and mortality remain what they were in 1933, the population would continue to increase slightly for seven years more and in 1943 would amount to 40,900,000. By 1981 it would be reduced to 34,300,000.[1] At the same time the population would age considerably. The young people under 20 years who in 1881 constituted 46·3 per cent. of the total population and in 1931 still 32·4 per cent. would in 1981 be reduced to 22·5 per

[1] See *London and Cambridge Economic Service, Special Memorandum*, No. 40, August 1935.

47

cent. The old people over 60, on the other hand, who in 1881 constituted 7·4 per cent. of the total population, and in 1931 11·6 per cent., would by 1981 have increased to 22·5 per cent. While the ratio of the people under 20 to the people over 60 was about 6:1 in 1881 and about 3:1 in 1931, it would be 1:1 in 1981.

Conditions in England are fairly representative of conditions in western and northern Europe, but reproduction is quite different in eastern Europe. Making a survey of all countries predominantly inhabited by whites we may distinguish three groups:

1. Soviet Russia, with nearly 175 million inhabitants. The net reproduction rate is enormous and probably as high as it ever was, since mortality has decreased at least as much as fertility.

2. Southern Europe (Portugal, Spain, Italy, the Balkan States), Poland, Lithuania, and Canada, with likewise nearly 175 million inhabitants. The net reproduction in each of these countries is less than half as high as in Russia and in some cases is very low.

3. Western, northern, and central Europe, the United States, Australia, and New Zealand, with about 370 million inhabitants. The population no longer reproduces itself.

The population of groups 2 and 3, which comprise Europe without Russia, the United States, Canada, and Oceania, increased in 1933 by about 3,500,000.

But this was not a genuine growth; it was due to a temporary age-composition which tends to swell the number of births and to reduce the number of deaths. If fertility and mortality remain constant, or if they both decrease to the same extent, the excess of births over deaths would be bound to decrease and would finally turn into an excess of deaths over births. Soviet Russia, on the other hand, where the population, according to official estimates, has increased in 1927–33 by 3 millions a year, has an enormous genuine population growth. If fertility and mortality there remain constant or decrease to the same extent, the population would go on increasing at a very rapid rate and thereby increase its share in the white population of the earth. If the population of Soviet Russia continues to grow as, according to the official figures, it has grown from 1924 till 1934, it would by the year 2000 amount to about 650 millions. If fertility and mortality remain in western and northern Europe what they were in 1933, the population which now is about 193 millions would reach its maximum of 196 or 197 millions in the late 1940's, and by the year 2000 would be reduced to about 150 millions.

In making these statements I am, of course, far from predicting anything. My object has been merely to show what would happen if fertility and mortality remain what they are to-day. This is a fundamental difference which is often overlooked. We should clearly distinguish between estimates meant to be forecasts, and computations which merely show what will be the trend of population on certain definite assumptions. To predict the actual population of Europe ten years from now would involve a risk which no serious statistician should be willing to shoulder; he need only remember that quite unexpectedly the population of Europe between 1914 and 1919 decreased by 12 millions. To compute with the best available methods what would be the population 100 years from now, if fertility and mortality remain what they are, is his legitimate task if by so doing he merely wants to elucidate the present balance of births and deaths.

III

i. POSSIBILITIES OF INCREASING REPRODUCTION

THE balance of births and deaths, even in England, looks favourable still for 1933, if one compares the crude birth-rate of 14·4 and the crude death-rate of 12·3. But if fertility and mortality remain constant the population will age, the birth-rate will decrease, and the death-rate will increase. Both rates will be 13·8 in 1943, from when on deaths will exceed births. Ultimately the birth- and death-rates will be 11·1 and 21·4 respectively.

But fertility and mortality may change. After having shown what would be the population trend in England if fertility and mortality remained what they were in 1933, Dr. Enid Charles has carried out a similar computation on the assumption that fertility from now on would be again what it was in 1931, i.e. 10 per cent. higher than in 1933, and if mortality in the course of the next 15 years would be reduced by nearly three-quarters for infants and by nearly one-half for all age groups from 1 to 70 years and after 15 years would remain constant. In this case the population would continue to increase for about 25 years more until 1962, when the birth- and death-rates would both be 12·7, from when on deaths would exceed births. Ultimately the birth- and death-rates would be 12·1 and 16·5 respectively. It may be surprising that with an increase of fertility by 10 per cent. and a halving of mortality under 70 years, the ultimate birth-rate would be only 9 per cent. higher than if fertility and mortality did not change. The explanation is to be found in the fact that with such an enormous fall of mortality the population would age so much that the proportion of women at child-bearing age would decrease.

The question then arises: how would a reduction of mortality affect reproduction, if fertility at the various ages remains what it is? In order to judge the situation correctly one must realize that only the reduction of the mortality of women till the end of the child-bearing age plays a role, since it is irrelevant for reproduction whether the women die immediately after the child-bearing period or whether they reach a much higher age. But it so happens that just in those countries with the lowest reproduction rates mortality of females under 50 has been reduced so much that the margin for further improvement is slight. In England, according to mortality for 1933, 907 out of 1,000 newly born girls reach the age of 15 and 788 the age of 50. The corresponding figures for New Zealand are 956 and 863. If no newly born girl died before having reached the age of 50, they would all live 35 years between the age of 15 and of 50. According to mortality for 1933 the average was

30·03 years in England and 32·17 years in New Zealand. In northern and western Europe as a whole the net reproduction rate was about 0·76 and the gross reproduction rate 0·9. If no girl died here before having passed through child-bearing age, the net reproduction rate would be 0·9; if mortality of females under 50 were reduced by one-half, the net reproduction rate would be 0·83. In countries where mortality under 50 is still high to-day the possibilities of an increase of reproduction through a reduction of mortality are greater. But taking the territory comprised by Western civilization as a whole, no marked increase of reproduction can possibly be expected from a reduction of mortality.

How could an increase of nuptiality affect reproduction? Most people believe that an increase of marriages would have a considerable effect. But here again they are the victims of an optical illusion. To marry is considered the normal fate of a girl. If people see a family in which all the daughters are married, they take this as a matter of course. But whenever they meet a healthy, good-looking woman of 35 who has not married, imagination begins to work, and when they think of the numerous girls in factories, shops, and offices they are apt to believe that a very large proportion of all girls do not marry at all. This conception, however, is disproved by statistics. Nuptiality, to be sure, is not equal in all countries. The percentage of spinsters among the females of 40–50 years oscillates between 1·3 in Bulgaria (1926) and 26·2 in Northern Ireland (1926). It amounted to 9·3 in the United States (1930), to 11·4 both in Germany (1925) and France (1926), to 17·5 in England (1931), and to 23·9 in Sweden (1931). For western and northern Europe as a whole it is safe to say that only about one-seventh of all girls remain unmarried. What would be the effect on reproduction if the girls who, according to present nuptiality, remain unmarried, married at the same ages as those who actually marry and displayed the same fertility after their wedding? It certainly would be wrong to assume that the gross reproduction rate would proportionally rise, that is to say from 0·9 to 1·05. It would be wrong because a number of children who are now born as illegitimate children of girls who remain unmarried would be born as legitimate children conceived either before or after the wedding. To the extent that this would be so, the reproduction rate would not be increased at all by universal marriage. Sterility, moreover, is probably more frequent among those who do not marry than among those who marry. Even with universal marriage the gross reproduction rate of western and northern Europe would not exceed 1, if fertility remained what it was in 1933.

We have seen that with fertility for 1933 the population of western and northern Europe would not reproduce itself even if no newly born girl died before having passed through child-bearing age. We now see that with fertility as of 1933 the population of western and northern Europe would at best hold its own even if no newly born girl died before having passed through child-bearing age and if none remained unmarried.

The conclusion which we have just reached, of course, does not imply that an approach to universal marriage would have no marked effect upon reproduction in any country of western and northern Europe. It might have a very marked effect in the Irish Free State and in Northern Ireland where the proportion of girls who do not marry is large and where at the same time the number of illegitimate children is small. The effect probably would be less conspicuous in Sweden where, with a low nuptiality, the proportion of illegitimate children is very high. It would be negligible in countries like France and Germany where nuptiality is high and the proportion of illegitimate children also is rather high. In such countries the number of births may increase temporarily if marriages are promoted—as has been done recently in Germany through the grant of loans —but marriages could not be kept permanently on a much higher level than formerly since, anyway, only a small proportion of girls remained unmarried.

It may be objected that promotion of marriages will tend to reduce the age at marriage and that early marriages are particularly apt to increase fertility. But great caution must be used in appraising the influence of the age at marriage upon fertility. Fecundity will be realized to the full if a woman all through her child-bearing period has intercourse with a procreative man and does nothing to prevent conception or to procure abortion. But this does not imply that, in order to realize fecundity to the full, intercourse must be started from the beginning of maturity. There are women who have children at 15 years and there are women who have children at 50 years, and many a woman might have a child either at 15 or at 50; but there have been hardly any women who actually had children both at 15 and 50 years. Of two equally fecund women who do nothing to prevent conception or to procure abortion and who have intercourse with procreative men, the one starting at the age of 17 and the other at 25, the first will bear children during a longer period than the second, but the difference will not amount to eight years; the first may have her last child, say, at 42 and the second at 47. The fact that in former times girls who married later used to have many fewer children than girls who married earlier was due, perhaps, not so much to their late marriage as to the state of hygiene and medicine which let them or their husbands become prematurely invalid or the victims of a fatal disease. With the progress of hygiene and medicine early marriage as a factor promoting fertility certainly has become less important.

But does not experience show that early marriages still to-day are much more fertile than late marriages? It does; and the German Statistical Office quite recently has published results of a very interesting investigation which convey some idea of the actual differences. After having ascertained that, with the fertility and mortality for 1933, the average number of legitimate children born to married women was 1·67, while 2·42 would have been necessary in order to assure the reproduction of the population, the Office shows that the average number for women marrying at 20 years was 2·25, at 25 years 1·69, at 30 years 1·33, and at 35 years 0·78.[1] This would indicate that girls marrying at 20 years have 33 per cent. more children than girls marrying at 25, 69 per cent. more children than those marrying at 30, and three times as many children as those marrying at 35. But the girls marrying at 30 years or more are numerically not very important, and the fact that the girls marrying at 20 had 33 per cent. more children than those marrying at 25 by no means proves that the girls who actually married at 25 would have had

[1] See *Sonderhefte zu Wirtschaft und Statistik*, No. 15, p. 78, Berlin, 1935.

33 per cent. more children if they had married at 20. It may well be, for example, that the girls who marry at 25 mostly belong to other social classes than those who marry at 20, and that many of them would not have had any more children if they had married at an earlier age.[1] A striking increase of fertility should not be expected from an increase in the number of marriages or from a change in the age at marriage.[2]

The decrease of fertility can be explained neither by a decrease of fecundity nor by a decrease of nuptiality nor by a rise of the age at marriage. Fertility has decreased through the spread of birth-control. If, as many people believe, birth-control were practised extensively only within certain classes of the population, reproduction could not possibly be as low as it is. The very fact that with present fertility in western and northern Europe a married woman passing through child-bearing age bears, on an average, two children only proves beyond any doubt that in the majority of the marriages birth-control

---

[1] It may be mentioned in this connexion that among the women enumerated on 16 June 1933 who had married in 1933, the percentage of women with no child by their present husband was only 69·2 for those who had married under 20 years, 77·0 for those who had married between 20 and 25 years, and 84·9 for those who had married between 25 and 30 years (see *Sonderhefte*, No. 15, p. 12).

[2] If with earlier marriages the number of children should not increase and the average age of mothers at birth should decrease, population decline might be accelerated because the mean length of a generation would be shortened.

must be practised successfully. A great and permanent rise of fertility, therefore, can be obtained only through a restriction of birth-control. Those who consider economic distress as the main cause of birth-control are inclined to assume that with a general improvement of economic conditions birth-control would be forgone by many couples. But the influence of prosperity and depression upon fertility in countries with extensive birth-control has so far manifested itself only inasmuch as the varying frequency of marriages has affected temporarily the speed at which fertility decreased. No one assumes that the well-to-do would have more children if they were wealthier still; why should the poor desire more children if they were better off?

Many measures have been adopted recently in Italy and Germany to increase the number of births. Italy[1] tried to discourage celibacy and childlessness and to encourage the raising of large families, by taxing bachelors and married couples with no or few children; by granting tax reductions and exemptions to State employees with at least 7 children and to other workers and employees with at least 10 children; by granting birth premiums and family allowances; by giving preference to married men or women with relatively large families in the allocation of places in

[1] See David Glass, *The Struggle for Population*, pp. 34–40, Oxford, 1936.

the central and local Government services, and in private enterprise, and also in the allocation of cheap houses and flats; and by providing a wide range of services for the protection of mothers and children. Italy introduced also severe laws against birth-control propaganda and deliberate abortion; she impeded the flow of labour from the country to the towns and initiated a movement in the reverse direction. But her efforts to increase the number of births were a complete failure. When this policy was inaugurated in 1926, the yearly births numbered 1,095,000. They have been below a million in every year since 1931.

Germany, in many respects, followed the example of Italy and, in addition, encouraged marriage and provided more employment for men by granting a loan when the woman to be married had been employed for at least nine months in the previous two years. But on the whole she relies much less on State action than Italy, and rightly expects a striking change in the trend of fertility rather from the spread of new ideals and a spontaneous desire of married couples to have numerous children. It is impossible to tell whether she will succeed in the long run. The results in the first three years are doubtful. The increase in the number of births was mainly due to an increase of first and second births. If it is true, as is claimed officially, that abortions have diminished conspicuously, the total number of births should have increased much more than it actually has, unless the use of other means of birth-control has expanded.

To increase fertility is a gigantic task. Fertility in the territory comprised by Western civilization is so low because most couples want few children. Even if the desire to raise children should not diminish further, fertility, as a whole, is bound to decrease as long as the most efficient birth-control devices are not universally known. A stop in the downward trend of fertility in the near future is to be expected only from an increasing desire to raise children, and a general desire for more children is hardly to be expected as long as public opinion in most countries does not favour population growth.

ii. POPULATION MOVEMENTS AND PUBLIC OPINION

The social, economic, and financial implications from a growing to an at first stationary, and later decreasing, population are manifold and few people so far realize the seriousness of the situation. This is quite surprising in itself, and it is the more surprising if one visualizes what, only twenty-five years ago, would have been the reaction of public opinion to the prospect of a population decrease in the near future. No one can doubt that such a prospect would have caused the greatest alarm.

Up to the World War practically all Governments

and the great majority of the people viewed a large and increasing population as an economic asset. The rise of the standard of living and of prosperity in general in countries like England, Germany, or the United States was largely attributed to the increasing number of consumers who, by their ever-increasing wants, widened the outlets for more intensive and therefore more economical production in agriculture and manufactures. The growth in the number of consumers seemed to be a necessary prerequisite for the development of natural resources and for progress in every branch of business. France, as a rule, was quoted as a typical example of a country which economically, and therefore also politically, lost ground as a consequence of her stationary population.

Since the World War many Governments and the majority of the people have taken an opposite viewpoint. A large and increasing population is no longer considered an economic asset but an economic burden. Unemployment, poverty, wars, and many other evils from which mankind suffers are attributed to over-population; if there were fewer people there would be no need for territorial expansion, every one might find work at home, and every one might get a larger share of the social product.

This radical change in public opinion from a desire for population growth to a fear of over-population occurred without a fundamental change in the economic system. I do not mean to say that striking, even sensational, economic events have not taken place in many countries in the last two decades; on the contrary these events have occurred, and in most cases have occurred so unexpectedly as to upset accepted ideas regarding prosperity and depression, as well as regarding their causes, and to obscure the fact that population growth or decline has certain definite and predictable economic consequences, regardless of the events which occur from time to time in the economico-political world. Unless such events give rise to profound and lasting changes in the economic system—a thing which we cannot perceive for western Europe and America over the last two decades—they will not, as a rule, exert marked influence upon the economic effects of population growth.

There are, I think, in the main, two reasons why so many people make great mistakes in appraising the economic effects of population movements. They look merely at the changes in the total number of inhabitants without examining the changes in the various age groups, and they consider only one effect, not being aware that every population movement has many far-reaching consequences. Let me illustrate this by a few examples:

In the course of 1915 people in Germany began to realize that, as a consequence of the War, deaths increased while births decreased, so that there was no longer an excess of births over deaths. This, they argued, must have an immediate influence upon the demand for new homes: 'Prior to the War, we had each year 800,000 more births than deaths; since there are on an average four persons per household we built, apart from replacement, 200,000 new lodgings to accommodate the yearly population growth of 800,000; what is the use of building new houses if the population decreases?' People simply could not be made to see that their conclusions were perfectly absurd; that it is not a quartette of newly born children who take a flat; that it is not the death of four soldiers which leaves a dwelling vacant; that the demand for lodgings depends mainly on the excess of newly created over dissolved households; and that the number of births and the number of dying soldiers have practically no influence upon the number of households created or dissolved. As a matter of fact, the number of households increased continuously during the War, and Germany consequently had for many years a terrible shortage of housing accommodation. The fact that there were so few births in 1915–19 will influence the German real estate market only around 1940, when the number of newly created households may be considerably smaller than heretofore and may for some years lag behind the number of dissolved households.

Another example. Some years ago, just before

sailing for America, I attended a public meeting on birth-control in Berlin. Unemployment had then reached a peak and a well-known economist said he could not understand how, in view of such a state of affairs, any one dared to question the necessity of more birth-control. The public could not understand it either, and applauded enthusiastically. A few days after my arrival in Washington, one of the most prominent American experts on labour problems said in a radio talk that people should not wonder at the large number of unemployed, in view of the ever-increasing population. It evidently has escaped the attention of many of those whose business it is to form public opinion that it is not the newly born children who crowd the labour market and that it is only a small proportion of the deceased who create occupational openings by their death. I even venture to say that if one set out to increase unemployment in a given country for the next fifteen years, one could find no more efficient means than birth-restriction on a very large scale.

Let us assume, for the sake of argument, that birth-restriction should go so far that no child would be born in that country during the next fifteen years. What would be the effect upon the labour market? Certainly, not a single man would find work more easily merely because no more children were being born. As a matter of fact the number of persons looking for a job would increase in the next fifteen years as in the past, because there would be more boys and girls reaching the bread-winning age than men and women leaving their jobs on account of old age, death, &c. The number of job-hunters might increase even more than before, because many young women who, if they had children, would not work might be looking for work if they had no children. What is still worse, the number of people thrown out of employment would increase at a terrific speed. The industries catering for the needs of the youngest children would be the first to be ruined. They would be followed by those supplying the wants of the older children, and so on. Teachers would lose employment, and so forth. It may seem at first sight as if the lack of children could not possibly reduce the national income and that, if the total purchasing power remained the same, industry as a whole would not be worse off. But with the increasing number of unemployed, wages and salaries would necessarily drop so that the national income and the demand for goods would decrease after all. Conditions might change again when, in fifteen years from now, labour would become scarce because there would not be any young people to fill the positions then becoming vacant by reason of disability or old age, just as lodgings may become vacant in Germany twenty years after the cradles were left empty.

Or take emigration, which just now is so often recommended as a means of reducing unemployment. Let us assume, for the sake of argument, that next year the population of England decreases by 10 per cent., say through the emigration of all people whose names begin with B. What would be the effect upon unemployment? Many people will say: unemployment would become negligible because (1) one-tenth of the unemployed has emigrated, (2) some of the employed remaining in the country would take the places of the shopkeepers, &c., who emigrated, (3) the unemployed whose names begin with A, C, &c., would get the jobs of the emigrated employees and of the employees mentioned under (2); the average standard of living would rise very much because (1) practically every one would have a job, (2) taxation would be lightened since unemployment assistance would become negligible, (3) the disappearance of one-tenth of domestic consumers would be offset by the increased purchasing power of the remaining nine-tenths and the increased exports of British goods due to the demand of those who have emigrated. But this argument entirely neglects the disharmonies created by an emigration of one-tenth of the population. The heaviest items of public expense—debt-service, defence, &c.—would not be lightened at all and would therefore involve a heavier *per capita* burden. One-tenth of the dwellings now occupied would become vacant, and real estate would fall in value. The building trades and all industries producing building material would be paralysed. Other trades supplying the bare necessities of life would suffer likewise. While unemployment doubtless would decrease in certain trades it would increase in others. Courageous statesmanship which would not be afraid of a radicalism unheard of in England might be able to remove the newly created disharmonies, but the sacrifices involved would perhaps not be smaller than those which would be necessary to solve the unemployment problem with the present population.

But no matter whether unemployment is actually due to over-population and can be cured by a reduction of population, no matter whether the sudden change in views on population trends in general was justified or not, it is a fact that public opinion in the countries of Western civilization, wherever it is free to express itself, approves of a policy restricting population growth.

Theoretically there exist four means for checking the population growth in an individual country: reduction of births, increase of deaths, promotion of emigration, and restriction of immigration. Some of these means are less popular than others. Ethical considerations prevent people from advocating an increase of mortality. National pride, and still more the difficulties of finding adequate countries to welcome the emigrants, interfere with the promotion of emigration. But national pride is not involved as long as emigration is confined to emigration into colonies, and in this case the opposition to immigration may be mitigated through subventions granted by the motherland. England has thus negotiated in 1925 a Migration and Settlement Agreement with the Commonwealth of Australia according to which the British Government is to pay £150,000 for every £750,000 of loan money issued by the Commonwealth Government and expended by the State Governments on approved schemes of development which tend, directly or indirectly, to increase the opportunities for the settlement of persons from the United Kingdom. Such schemes may be indeed mutually advantageous, but they are particularly favoured by people who believe that the present unemployment in England is largely due to the decrease of emigration in post-War years. The naïvety of this belief has been strikingly exposed in the recent Report of the Inter-Departmental Committee on Migration Policy:

'We have seen it stated that the volume of migration since the War has fallen short of the volume of migration in the corresponding period prior to the War by a number equivalent to the total present number of unemployed persons in this country: whence the conclusion is drawn that if migration from the United Kingdom had continued at the same rate since the War as before the War, there would be no unemployment in the United Kingdom to-day. In fact the total volume of migration in the 15 years from 1919 to 1933 falls short by only 533,000 of the total estimated volume of migration in the 15 years 1899 to 1913. Even if, however, the position were as stated, and if the volume of migration in the last 15 years had been increased by some $2\frac{1}{2}$ million, it seems to us to be probable, if not certain, that the economic condition of the Dominions would, as a result, have been materially worse than it is now, in which case the burden of unemployment in this country might well have been increased rather than reduced.'[1]

It does not at all seem to me 'to be probable, if not certain', that the economic condition of the Dominions would, as a result of a so much larger immigration from England, have been materially worse than it is now, and it was surprising to find such a statement in a report signed in August 1934 by the chairman of the Committee, Mr. Malcolm MacDonald, who on the second of that month had declared that Australia's population was destined to grow in the comparatively near future to 40 or 50 millions. But the refutation of the fallacy that unemployment in England would now be much smaller if emigration since the War had been the same as before the War was most timely. It seems, however, so far not to have been heeded

[1] *Report to the Secretary of State for Dominion Affairs of the Inter-Departmental Committee on Migration Policy*, 1934, pp. 34-5.

sufficiently. I shall confine myself to quoting the statement made in November 1934 in the House of Commons that members were 'apt to overlook the fact that but for the closing of the avenues of emigration throughout the Empire there would have been little or no unemployment problem at all in this country'. This speaker evidently believed that if the avenues of emigration in the Empire had not been closed, several million more people (the bulk of the unemployed with their wives and children) would have emigrated to and stayed in the Dominions and colonies. The fallacy of this argument will be perhaps best appraised if one realizes that emigrants of British nationality to the overseas territories of the Empire in 1919–29 averaged 130,000, that is, more than in any year prior to 1906. Since 1929 British emigration to the Empire has been very small; as a matter of fact outward migration has been much smaller than inward migration. No one can tell what would have been the size of emigration if the Dominions had not restricted immigration. In view of the economic depression overseas, which is reflected also in the large number of those who returned to Europe, it is hard to see how those restrictions could have affected essentially the number of unemployed in this country.[1] But whether emigration

[1] The proportion of British born, and especially English born, living in the non-European parts of the Empire is often very much

is a remedy for unemployment or not, public opinion in England favours emigration and thereby tends to accelerate the process of population decrease. In most other countries, however, the promotion of emigration is not popular, and public opinion there has concentrated on the two other means of checking population growth: restriction of births and restriction of immigration.

Birth-control and restriction of immigration were advocated, of course, by quite a few people long before the World War, but they were advocated only by certain classes or groups of people, and they were not recommended as a means of checking population growth. Working-men in the United States, for instance, demanded the restriction of immigration merely in order to lessen the inflow of foreigners who were willing to work for low wages. Liberally minded people in all countries demanded freedom of birth-control merely in order to give individual women a chance to avoid pregnancies which, for one reason or another, would be detrimental to them. Immediately after the War immigration restriction

over-estimated. The number of persons born in England and Wales and living in Canada was 530,000 in 1911, 700,000 in 1921, and nearly 750,000 in 1931; in Australia it was 360,000 in 1911, 460,000 in 1921, and 500,000 in 1933. The maximum for all overseas territories of the Empire was probably reached in 1929 when it was something like 1,700,000. Since then it may have decreased by about 100,000.

became popular with the ruling classes in the United States, because it offered a convenient method of excluding the politically undesirable foreigner. But in the United States, as practically everywhere, public opinion now favours immigration restriction as a sure method of checking population increase, and the same motive has created a sympathetic attitude towards birth-control among many people who would scorn the idea of being liberally minded.

Public opinion became opposed to population growth without a fundamental change in the economic system, and at a time when the rate of population increase had already slowed down. Public opinion, moreover, has not been disturbed at all by the fact that the slowing down of the population increase has brought no economic relief, while population growth, when it was large, was accompanied by a general rise in the standard of living. All this may seem surprising, but it is not so. It is an easy matter to convince the man-in-the-street that restriction of immigration diminishes unemployment, and that unemployment would be still larger if immigration were not restricted. It is an easy matter likewise to convince him that since those who have only one child are better off than those who have three or more children it must mean general economic relief if there are fewer children. But this does not imply that the arguments against population growth are sounder than the arguments in favour of population growth. Unemployment may be the result of under-population and not of over-population. Birth-control may be beneficial for the individual and at the same time detrimental to society.

I may be asked at this point: how is it possible that fewer children would not mean general economic relief when we see in daily life that those who have only, say, one child can afford to live better than those who have three or more children? My answer to this question is very simple. Mr. Smith, the real estate agent, is economically better off with one child than with more children as long as other people have more children. But if the rest of the community had one child per family, Mr. Smith would starve because there would be much less demand for new buildings. A man may live comfortably from a business which depends mainly on the increase of population even if he himself does not contribute to that increase. But he can do this only as long as others do not follow his example. It may seem at first sight as if real estate were an exceptional case. But is there any line of business in such countries as England or the United States that is not carried on on the assumption that population will continue to increase?

Birth-control and immigration restriction have been applied, for instance, in the United States with ever-increasing intensity. The result has been a slowing down of population increase which, if fertility and mortality remain what they are, will lead finally to a decrease in numbers. But it seems doubtful whether the prevailing population trend will actually bring about economic relief. The people who appear to be most in need of economic relief are the farmers. But the plight of the American farmers is that they produce much more food than the 128 million inhabitants of the United States can possibly consume. They find, of course, a partial outlet by selling abroad, but food exports have become more and more difficult on account of the large number of food exporting countries all over the world and of the more or less successful attempts of some grain-importing countries to increase home production.

Even if immigration restriction benefited the American working-man and birth-control benefited the American family as much as the most fervent advocates of immigration restriction and of birth-control make out, there would still remain the incontrovertible fact that the American farmer would be better off if there were now 145 millions within the Union instead of 128. But public opinion in America, and even public opinion in Europe, is convinced that the immigration restriction policy has done more good than harm to the United States. Few people, I think, on either side of the Atlantic are aware how completely they have changed their opinion in this matter. Immigration into the United States immediately before the World War was larger than ever before. It reached its peak as late as 1913. No one in Europe doubted that it was an ideal situation for the United States to have a yearly influx of a million workers whose cost of upbringing had been borne by other nations. When Americans boasted of their high standard of living, of the chances every one had to become economically independent and you told them that Europe paid part of the bill, they answered, slightly embarrassed: 'We are not responsible for this state of affairs; it is not the pull on our side but the push on your side which brings your people into our country; moreover, your emigrants are not a sheer loss, you get considerable remittances from many of them.' But they did not deny that immigration on a large scale was indispensable for their prosperity. Were we all wrong, then, or can it be, after all, that without any fundamental change in the economic system conditions have changed so much that what was true twenty years ago is utterly false to-day?

In order to be able to answer this and similar questions we ought to know much more than we actually do about the social, economic, and financial consequences of population movements. Thorough research work is needed along all these lines. Let me mention as an illustration a series of problems which should be studied with regard to the financial consequences of the present population trend:

To what extent will the decrease in the proportion of children increase the adults' capacity to pay taxes? To what extent will it reduce public expenses (for schools, welfare institutions, &c.)?

To what extent will the increase in the proportion of old people unable to earn a living increase public expenses (for old-age pensions, &c.)? To what extent will additional public expenses be caused by the fact that with the decrease of fertility old people unable to earn a living will, in fewer cases than in the past, have children to support them?

To what extent will the changes in the demand for various goods (fewer 'cradles', more 'coffins') affect tax receipts? To what extent will the reduction of house building activity and the slackening of speculation in urban real estate affect tax receipts?

To what extent will the capacity to meet obligations contracted in the past be affected (civil and military pensions, long-term loans)? To what extent has the present population trend to be taken into account when issuing new long-term loans and fixing the terms of amortization?

The basic data for the measurement of present population trends are available for most of the countries predominantly inhabited by whites, and such measurement does not presuppose a command of higher mathematics or a special training of any kind but merely the knowledge of a few very simple devices. On the other hand, it is as yet impossible to make a comprehensive scientific appraisal of the social, economic, and financial effects of the marked change in the population trend within the countries of Western civilization. The relations of population growth and decrease to economic pressure and relief are more complicated than most people realize. These relations are complicated for no other reason than because social and economic life is complicated, and they can be elucidated only through a series of very careful and thorough investigations. As matters stand I can only say this much: it is a one-sided view to denounce population growth as the root of all evil and to praise birth-restriction and other means of checking population growth as the surest method to secure general economic relief.

If fertility and mortality remain constant or decrease to the same extent and if no conspicuous immigration takes place, we shall soon witness in England, as in most other countries of Western civilization, a steady decrease in the population as a whole. At the same time, every branch of industry is still carried on on the assumption that the population will continue to increase. This does not, of course, imply that every branch of industry will suffer from a reduction in the total number of consumers. But people should realize that a change in the population trend is, under any circumstances, a serious matter with far-reaching consequences, good and bad. If leading men and women continue to talk and act as if such a change had not occurred, or welcome it naïvely as an all-round blessing, the frictions caused by unavoidable displacements and shifts will be most painful. If readjustment takes place in time, the detrimental effects of the change in population trends may be minimized.

APPENDIX

DISTRIBUTION OF RACES IN AFRICA, AMERICA, AND OCEANIA

In discussing our knowledge of the population of the earth, we made some estimates of the number of whites (of European stock) in Africa, America, and Oceania, and of the number of negroes (of African stock) in America. These estimates were based as far as possible on the censuses of the various countries. Most of these censuses contain some data bearing on the race composition of the population, but very few of the published data are comparable with one another.

The censuses of some countries, such as the Union of South Africa and the United States of America, tend to restrict the number of whites by narrowing the definition of the term. In the Union of South Africa the census distinguishes the following races :[1]

1. European or White Persons: persons of pure European descent.[2]
2. Asiatics: persons born of, or descended from, races belonging to the continent of Asia, including Parsees and Syrians.
3. Natives: pure-blooded aboriginals of the Bantu race.
4. Coloured Persons.

The policy of the Union of South Africa is thus to segregate three groups of pure-blooded persons (Europeans, Asiatics, Bantus), and to combine in a fourth group (Coloured

---

[1] See *Census of the Population of the Union of South Africa 1921*, *Report*, pp. 10, 26, Pretoria, 1924.

[2] This includes, of course, persons of pure European descent born in continents other than Europe.

Persons) all pure-blooded persons who are neither Europeans nor Asiatics nor Bantus, and all persons of mixed races.

In the United States the census (1930) distinguishes the following races: White, Negro, Mexican, Indian, Chinese, Japanese, Filipino, Hindu, Korean, Hawaiian, Malay, Siamese, Samoan. The instructions to the enumerators read:[1]

151. Negroes.—A person of mixed white and Negro blood should be returned as a Negro, no matter how small the percentage of Negro blood. Both black and mulatto persons are to be returned as Negroes, without distinction. A person of mixed Indian and Negro blood should be returned a Negro, unless the Indian blood predominates and the status as an Indian is generally accepted in the community.

152. Indians.—A person of mixed white and Indian blood should be returned as Indian, except where the percentage of Indian blood is very small, or where he is regarded as a white person by those in the community where he lives. (See par. 151 for mixed Indian and Negro.)

154. Mexicans.—Practically all Mexican laborers are of a racial mixture difficult to classify, though usually well recognized in the localities where they are found. In order to obtain separate figures for this racial group, it has been decided that all persons born in Mexico, or having parents born in Mexico, who are not definitely white, Negro, Indian, Chinese, or Japanese, should be returned as Mexican.

155. Other mixed races.—Any mixture of white and nonwhite should be reported according to the nonwhite parent. Mixtures of colored races should be reported according to the race of the father, except Negro-Indian (see par. 151).

The policy of the United States, then, is to assign each person, whether pure-blooded or not, to a specific race,[2] the

---

[1] *Census of the United States 1930, Population*, vol. ii, pp. 1398–9.

[2] The 1890 census was the last one to classify the persons of

allocation of persons of mixed race being influenced by political considerations. Any mixture of white and non-white is reported according to the non-white parent, but a person of mixed white and Indian blood is counted as white, if the percentage of Indian blood is very small or if he is regarded as a white person by those in the community where he lives; if, however, such a person is born in Mexico or has parents born in Mexico, he is counted as Mexican, unless he is 'definitely' white or Indian. Mixtures of coloured races are reported according to the race of the father, but a person of mixed Indian and negro blood is counted as negro unless the Indian blood predominates and the status as an Indian is generally accepted in the community.

The term 'white' is used in the United States in a broader sense than in the Union of South Africa. In the Union only persons of European descent are counted as whites, white persons of races belonging to the continent of Asia being counted as Asiatics and white persons of races belonging to other continents being counted as coloured. In the United States all pure white persons are counted as whites no matter whether they are of European, Asiatic, or African

African descent according to the degrees of coloured blood. The instruction to the enumerators then read: 'Be particularly careful to distinguish between blacks, mulattoes, quadroons, and octoroons. The word "black" should be used to describe those persons who have three-fourths or more black blood; "mulatto", those persons who have from three-eighths to five-eighths black blood; "quadroon", those persons who have one-fourth black blood; and "octoroon", those persons who have one-eighth or any trace of black blood.' (See Carroll D. Wright, *The History and Growth of the United States Census*, 56th Congress, 1st Session, Senate Document No. 194, p. 187, Washington, 1900.)

descent.[1] But here, as in the Union, hardly any but pure whites are to be counted as whites.

In the Latin countries of America and in the colonies of Latin nations the line between whites and coloured is not drawn so sharply. According to the Mexican census of 1921 the whites constituted 10 per cent. of the non-foreign population,[2] and according to an estimate based on the Mexican census of 1930, 15 per cent.[3] On the other hand, only 3·7 per cent. of the persons born in Mexico and living in 1930 in the United States were whites according to the standard of the latter country.[4]

The censuses for French colonies usually distinguish merely 'Europeans and Assimilated' (*Européens et assimilés*) and 'Natives' (*Indigènes*). Even this distinction is by no means uniform. The 'Europeans and Assimilated' sometimes comprise only persons of European descent, sometimes (on the Somali coast) all non-natives (including thus Asiatics, &c.), sometimes (Réunion) all persons of European stock and all natives (excluding thus only Asiatics, &c.).

It is evident that in most countries inhabited by several races there are numerous individuals who cannot be included

[1] Prior to 1930 Mexicans (unless they were pure Indians) were counted as whites.

[2] See *Resumen del Censo General de Habitantes de 30 de Noviembre de 1921*, p. 62. Out of a total population of 14,334,780, there were 1,404,718 white Mexicans and 101,958 foreigners of all races.

[3] See *Statesman's Year-Book*, 1935, p. 1117. Out of a total population of 16,553,398, there were 2,444,466 white Mexicans and 159,876 foreigners of all races.

[4] See *Census of the United States 1930, Population*, vol. ii, p. 231. Of the 641,462 persons returned as born in Mexico 23,743 were returned as whites.

with certainty in either race, and the difficulty of allocating
borderland cases has induced many countries to forgo altogether the distinction by races and to ascertain merely the
nationality and the country of birth. The censuses of such
countries, of course, do not provide a direct insight into the
race composition of the population, and great caution must
be observed in drawing conclusions on race from figures
relating to nationality or country of birth. Such figures, as
a matter of fact, tell practically nothing about the race composition of the population of a country like the Union of
South Africa, because the fact that a person is of South
African nationality and born in South Africa does not indicate
at all to which race he belongs. In a country like Egypt, with
a not homogeneous native population and a great variety of
foreigners, it is very difficult, to be sure, to estimate the
number of persons of European descent from the data on
nationality and country of birth, because it is impossible to
say, for example, how many persons of European descent are
among the Egyptians born in Egypt, among the French born
in Algeria, among the Italians born in Tripoli, &c. But since
the number of persons of European descent among the
Egyptians born in Egypt is probably rather small, and since
the foreigners in Egypt constitute only 1·6 per cent. of the
total population, the data on nationality and country of birth
provide after all the basis for a rough estimate of the total
number of persons of European descent. In colonies, finally,
where there are hardly any white settlers, it is comparatively
easy to derive the approximate number of persons of European descent from the data on nationality and country of
birth.

The statistics of races are, then, in a rather chaotic state, and totals arrived at by indiscriminately adding the official figures, for example, of 'Europeans' in African colonies are most misleading.[1] But the inadequacy of the official statistics is not the only reason why recent attempts to show the race composition of various continents have been inadequate. The following table shows the results of the investigations of two prominent experts on race distribution in America:

				Willcox[2]	Loyo[3]
Whites .	.	.		140,000,000	166,152,397
Indians	.	.		14,400,000	17,226,722
Mestizos	.	.		18,000,000	38,583,925
Negroes	.	.			20,683,596
Mulattos	.	.		} 66,600,000[4]	7,630,879
Others .	.	.			865,345
	Total	.		239,000,000	251,521,224[5]

[1] One example may serve as an illustration. According to the French official statistics (see Statistique générale de la France, *Résultats statistiques du recensement général de la population*, 1931, vol. i, part i, p. 113), there were in the French non-Mediterranean colonies in Africa 326,654 'Europeans and Assimilated', but this number includes among others 192,961 inhabitants of Réunion, the majority of whom are coloured of African descent, and 89,900 inhabitants of French West Africa, three-quarters of whom are natives with French citizenship.

[2] See *International Migrations*, vol. ii, pp. 78, 81, 82. Figures refer to 1929.

[3] See Gilberto Loyo, *La Política Demográfica de México*, Table following p. 482, Mexico, 1935. Figures refer to 1930-2.

[4] This figure is not given by Willcox. We have derived it by subtracting his figures for whites, Indians, and mestizos from his total.

[5] Including 378,360 for Newfoundland, U.S. Virgin Islands, British Honduras, and French Guiana, not distributed by races.

APPENDIX

The totals for whites were arrived at as follows (in thousands):

	Willcox		Loyo	
	Whites	*Total*	*Whites*	*Total*
United States of America	95,800	120,013	110,375	122,775
Canada, Newfoundland .	8,900	9,786	10,242[1]	10,673
Mexico . . .	2,700	14,335	2,483	16,525
Cuba	2,100	3,569	2,694	3,962
Rest of North and Centr. A.	300	13,779	2,844	14,386
South America . .	30,200	76,850	37,512	82,879
Total .	140,000	238,332	166,152	251,200

Willcox's figures for whites in North America are far too low. For the United States he apparently entered by mistake an estimate for 1921. In the case of Canada and Newfoundland he must have made a similar mistake since here again the difference between his figures for the whites and the total population is too high. In estimating the number of whites in the 'rest' of North and Central America at 300,000 he must have overlooked that this territory includes, for example, Puerto Rico with over 1,000,000 whites. But even if one raises his total for whites in North and Central America from 109·8 millions to 125 millions, the acceptance of his figures for Indians and mestizos in all America (32·4 millions) would imply that the negroes and mulattos in all America numbered nearly 50 millions, which seems far too high a figure.

Loyo's investigation is much more ambitious. He gives for practically each country or colony the number of whites,

[1] Excluding Newfoundland.

Indians, mestizos, negroes, mulattos, Chinese, Japanese, and other Asiatics. His method is defective mainly in two respects :

1. He adds the official figures of the various countries indiscriminately and does not, for example, take account of the fact that in the United States statistics all persons with a trace of negro blood are entered as negroes. He thus arrives at a total of 20,684,000 negroes and 7,631,000 mulattos, while if for the United States he had counted 60 per cent. as mulattos (which certainly would have been a most conservative estimate) he would have obtained a total of 13,331,000 negroes and 14,984,000 mulattos.

2. He resorts to estimates in cases where there is no need for it. He thus assumes[1] that of the total population of the United States, 89·9 were whites, 0·2 per cent. Indians, 9·9 per cent. negroes, 0·1 per cent. Chinese, and 0·1 per cent. Japanese. His figures compare with the official figures as follows :

			Loyo	Official
Whites .	.	.	110,374,766	108,864,207
Indians	.	.	245,550	332,397
Mestizos	.	.	..	1,422,533[2]
Negroes	.	.	12,254,729[3]	11,891,143
Chinese	.	.	122,775	74,954
Japanese	.	.	122,775	138,834
Others .	.	.	..	50,978
	Total	.	122,775,046	122,775,046

In other cases estimates, of course, were indispensable,

[1] See Table following p. 485.   [2] Mexicans.

[3] This figure apparently should read 11,909,180 (9·9 per cent. of 122,775,046 are 12,154,730, and Loyo evidently meant to allocate 9·7 and not 9·9 per cent. to negroes).

and estimates of an expert such as Loyo are most welcome. But it is strange in how many cases he under-estimates the number of negroes or mulattos. He thus counts for the Panama Canal Zone, the Bermudas, and Trinidad and Tobago, which all have a majority of negroes (including mulattos), not more than 6·8, 0, and 6 per cent. respectively.

Tables I–V contain estimates of the number of whites (of European descent) in Africa for 1835 and 1935, of the number of whites and negroes (including mulattos) in America for 1835, of the number of whites, negroes, Indians (including mestizos), and others in America for 1935, and of the number of whites, natives (including half-castes), and others in Oceania for 1935.

In studying these tables the reader should keep in mind:

1. The figures for whites in the various countries and colonies are not strictly comparable with one another. In many cases we have accepted the official figures although we are fully aware that while, for example, in the United States, few people who are not of pure European descent are counted as whites, this number is considerable, for example, in the Union of South Africa where many coloured people are counted as whites, and is still larger in the former and present Spanish and Portuguese colonies. Moreover, some of our figures for whites include whites of Asiatic descent, while most do not.

2. In a number of cases the figures for the total population, and still more so those for the various races, are estimates which may differ considerably from the truth.

3. The totals given in the tables are the sums of figures which do not all relate to the same date.

POPULATION MOVEMENTS

Our main conclusions are:

I. Africa 1835. The number of whites was about 135,000.

This figure is meant to exclude the army and navy. The European military population, excl. Algeria, was probably about 9,000; the number of European troops in Algeria may have been considerable.[1] Our total of 132,205 for the civil population is not all-inclusive, since it does not comprise Mozambique, the Spanish *presidios* in Morocco with numerous convicts, the other Spanish and the Danish and Dutch colonies; on the other hand, it shows for some important colonies figures of a later date than 1835, for example, for the Cape Colony the population as of 31 December 1837, which exceeded that of 1835.

II. Africa, 31 December 1935. The number of whites was about 4,000,000.

In making the entries for whites we have excluded, as far as possible, the army and navy. The number of European troops still included is too small to affect the total of 4,000,000.

The table on page 91 shows the number of whites in 1835 and 1935 by geographical divisions. It appears that on the African continent, excluding the Mediterranean countries and the South, i.e. in a territory considerably larger than Europe, the number of whites was about 1,000 in 1835 and about 100,000 in 1935.

III. America 1835. The number of whites was about 18,600,000, and the number of negroes about 9,800,000.

We have segregated, as far as possible, the number of troops from Europe, because they constitute in some colonies a considerable part of the white population.

[1] See Malte-Brun, *Géographie complète de la France et de ses colonies*, p. 452, Paris, 1857: 'The effectives of the army employed in Algeria vary according to the political circumstances; it numbered 21,511 men in 1832, and was brought to 105,000 men in 1846 . . .' These figures, of course, include native troops.

APPENDIX

Whites in Africa 1835 and 1935

Geographical Divisions	Sq. miles	1835	1935
Mediterranean countries* .	2,168,000	20,000	1,660,000
Union of South Africa . .	472,000	66,000	1,950,000
Rest of South Africa† . .	1,884,000	3,000	190,000
Rest of the continent . .	6,798,000	1,000	100,000
Islands	242,000	45,000	100,000
Total	11,564,000	135,000	4,000,000

* Egypt, Libya, Tunis, Algeria, Moroccos, Spanish Northern Africa, Tangier.

† Angola, South-West Africa, the Rhodesias, Nyasaland, Bechuanaland, Basutoland, Swaziland, Mozambique.

IV. America, 31 December 1935. The number of whites was about 172,000,000, the number of Indians about 53,000,000, and the number of negroes about 39,500,000.

There were besides about 1,400,000 'Others' who were nearly all Asiatics (Chinese, Japanese, East Indians, &c.).

The following table shows the number of whites and negroes in North, Central, and South America in 1835 and 1935.

White and Negro Population in America 1835 and 1935

Geographical Divisions	White		Negro	
	1835	1935	1835	1935
North America .	13,800,000	124,300,000	2,600,000	12,400,000
Central America	1,900,000	6,900,000	2,700,000	8,400,000
South America .	2,900,000	40,900,000	4,500,000	18,700,000
Total	18,600,000	172,100,000	9,800,000	39,500,000

V. Oceania, 31 December 1935. The number of whites was about 8,300,000[1] and the number of natives about 1,700,000.

There were besides about 400,000 'Others' (mostly Asiatics).

[1] The number of whites in 1835 was about 120,000; see p. 8.

TABLE I. *Whites in Africa about 1835*

| Countries | Year | Population | |
		Civil	Military
Egypt	1835	5,000	—
Morocco	1835	500	—
British Colonies:			
Cape of Good Hope . . .	1837	68,148	1,962
Mauritius	1835	15,000	1,376
Seychelles	1825	582	—
St. Helena	1836	2,200	473
West Coast	1838	500	712
French Colonies:			
Algeria	1835	11,221	..
Senegal	1836	195	376
Madagascar	1838	29	51
Bourbon (Réunion) . . .	1836	24,000	667
Portuguese Colonies:			
Cape Verde Is. and Guinea . .	1834	2,900	574
St. Thomé and Principe Is. . .	1844	100	160
Angola	1844	1,830	1,606
Total		132,205	7,957

The sign '—' indicates nil, the sign '..' unknown.

SOURCES FOR TABLE I

Egypt. See Adriano Balbi, 'L'Egitto', *Gazzetta di Milano*, July 1836, reprinted in Balbi, *Scritti geografici, statistici e vari*, vol. iii, p. 4, Torino, 1841.

Morocco. See Balbi, 'Cenni sulla regione Sahara-Atlante', *Gazzetta di Milano*, June 1836, reprinted in *Scritti geografici*, &c., vol. ii, p. 302.

Cape of Good Hope. See for civilians, Cape of Good Hope, *Blue Book 1837*, pp. 198–9. The number is not known for 1829–36. *Blue Book 1828*, pp. 242–3, gives for 1828, 55,355

Whites. The population figures do not include the resident strangers, some of whom were Whites. See for troops, 1 Jan. 1838, *Parliamentary Papers 1837–8*, vol. 37, p. 133.

Mauritius. In 1827 there were 8,111 Whites and 15,444 Free Coloured (see Robert Montgomery Martin, *Statistics of the Colonies of the British Empire*, p. 503, London, 1839). In 1835 there were 29,612 Whites and Free Coloured (see *Parliamentary Papers 1837–8*, vol. 47, p. 492). Martin, *Statistics of the Colonies* (1839), 'Statistical Chart', gives 15,000 Whites. Moreau de Jonnès, *Recherches statistiques sur l'esclavage colonial*, pp. 43–4, Paris, 1842, gives for 1832, 16,000 Whites. These figures probably do not include the aliens and resident strangers, who in 1836 included 670 European aliens (see Martin, *Statistics of Colonies*, p. 503). See for troops, 1 Jan. 1836, *Parliamentary Papers 1837–8*, vol. 37, pp. 134–5.

Seychelles. See Martin, *Statistics of Colonies*, p. 519. The troops are apparently included in the figures for Mauritius (see ibid., 'Statistical Chart').

St. Helena. See for estimate of civilians, Martin, *Statistics of Colonies*, p. 522; for troops, 1 Jan. 1837, *Parliamentary Papers 1837–8*, vol. 37, pp. 134–5.

West Coast. Martin, *Statistics of Colonies*, pp. 537, 553, 'Chart', gives for Sierra Leone, 1836: 105; Gambia, 1836: 43; Cape Coast Castle, 10; Accra, 5; Dix Cove, 1; Annamaboe, 2. He further states: 'In the aggregate we may estimate the number of British subjects, on the western coast of Africa, at about 50,000, of whom but 500 are Europeans.' For troops, 1 Jan. 1838, see *Parliamentary Papers 1837–8*, vol. 37, p. 133.

Algeria. See René Ricoux, *La démographie figurée de l'Algérie*, p. 33, Paris, 1880.

Senegal. See *Annales maritimes et coloniales 1838*, part ii, vol. i, pp. 630–1. Data refer to 31 Dec. 1836; the civil population includes fifty-one officials and their families.

Madagascar. See *Notices statistiques sur les colonies françaises*, vol. iv (1840), pp. 30, 34–6, 158–9. The civil population includes sixteen officials.

Bourbon. The number of white residents was 18,125 in 1826 (see Thomas, *Essai de statistique sur l'île de Bourbon*, MS. quoted in *Annales maritimes et coloniales 1828*, part ii, vol. ii, pp. 375–6), and 29,181 on 31 Dec. 1843 (see *Tableaux de population 1843*, p. 30). For the intervening period we have found the following estimates:

1827: 20,000; Moreau de Jonnès, p. 23.

1836: More than two-thirds of the total free population (39,817 incl. officials and troops); *Notices statistiques sur les colonies françaises*, vol. ii (1838), pp. 26, 30, 34–5.

1838: 20,000; Moreau de Jonnès, p. 24.

For the number of officials (125) and troops (667), see *Notices statistiques*, vol. ii (1838), p. 35.

Cape Verde Islands and Guinea. José Joaquim Lopes de Lima (*Ensaios sobre a Statistica das Possessões Portuguezas na Africa Occidental*, &c., Book I, part i, pp. 1, 6, 69A, Lisbon, 1844) gives 55,833 as population of the Cape Verde Islands according to the census of 1834, estimates the total population of the establishments in Portuguese Guinea at 4,500 incl. troops, and gives 574 as the strength of the troops of the entire colony on 31 Dec. 1843. He estimates the ratio of Whites to Coloured for the entire colony at 1 : 20.

St. Thomé and Principe Islands. Lopes de Lima (*Ensaios*, Book II, part i, pp. 2A, 52A, 52B) gives for 1844 as number of Whites and Mulattos in St. Thomé Island 47, and in Principe Island 138, and as troops 80 in each island.

Angola. Lopes de Lima (*Ensaios*, Book III, part i, pp. 4A, 139, Lisbon, 1846) gives as number of Whites 1,830, and as number of troops in 1845, 1,606. João de Andrado de Corvo (*Estudos sobre as Provincias Ultramarinas*, vol. i, p. 206, Lisbon, 1883) indicates that the figure of 1,830 refers to 1844. Recent official statistics (see Colónia de Angola, *Boletim Trimestral da Repartição Central de Estatística Geral 1934*, p. 114) date it, probably wrongly, as of 1846.

APPENDIX

TABLE II. *White and Total Population in Africa about 1935*

Countries		White Population		Total Population	
		Date	Number	Date	Number
Algeria	French	30 June 1934	900,000	30 June 1934	6,910,000
Angola	Port.	31 Dec. 1933	58,698	31 Dec. 1933	3,098,281
Basutoland	Brit.	1934	2,000	31 Dec. 1934	570,000
Bechuanaland	Brit.	1934	1,660	31 Dec. 1933	160,000
Belgian Congo	Belg.	1 Jan. 1935	17,845	31 Dec. 1934	9,300,836
Cameroons	Br. M.	31 Dec. 1934	316	31 Dec. 1934	778,352
Cameroons	Fr. M.	31 Dec. 1934	2,047	31 Dec. 1934	2,230,201
Cape Verde Islands	Port.	1933	854	31 Dec. 1933	160,000
Egypt		30 June 1934	200,000	30 June 1934	15,230,000
Eritrea	Ital.	21 Apr. 1931	4,560	31 Dec. 1933	600,000
Ethiopia		30 June 1935	3,000	31 Dec. 1933	5,500,000
French Equat. Africa	French	1 July 1931	4,591	1934	3,430,000
French West Africa	French	31 Dec. 1934	18,631	31 Dec. 1934	14,456,740
Gambia	Brit.	31 Dec. 1933	250	31 Dec. 1933	208,094
Gold Coast	Brit.	30 June 1934	2,400	30 June 1934	3,116,265
Kenya	Brit.	31 Dec. 1934	17,501	31 Dec. 1934	3,094,279
Liberia		1933	150	31 Dec. 1933	2,500,000
Libya	Ital.	21 Apr. 1931	49,407	31 Dec. 1933	720,000
Madagascar incl. dep.	French	31 Dec. 1933	24,610	31 Dec. 1933	3,820,987
Mauritius and dep.	Brit.	31 Dec. 1934	700	31 Dec. 1934	404,190
Morocco	French	31 Dec. 1933	160,000	31 Dec. 1933	5,500,000
Morocco	Span.	1933	32,804	1933	720,273
Mozambique	Port.	1935	23,131	1935	4,006,001
Nigeria	Brit.	23 Apr. 1931	4,674	31 Dec. 1933	19,349,921
Northern Africa	Span.	31 Dec. 1933	90,000	31 Dec. 1933	115,000
Northern Rhodesia	Brit.	31 Dec. 1934	11,464	31 Dec. 1934	1,378,490
Nyasaland	Brit.	31 Dec. 1934	1,800	31 Dec. 1934	1,603,914
Portuguese Guinea	Port.	1930	1,226	31 Dec. 1933	380,000
Réunion	French	31 Dec. 1933	70,000	31 Dec. 1933	200,000
Rio de Oro incl. Ifni	Span.	31 Dec. 1930	300	31 Dec. 1933	20,000
Ruanda-Urundi	Bel. M.	1 Jan. 1935	868	1 Jan. 1935	3,293,269
St. Helena and dep.	Brit.	31 Dec. 1934	400	31 Dec. 1934	4,397
St. Thomé, Principe	Port.	1921	1,115	31 Dec. 1933	60,000
Seychelles	Brit.	31 Dec. 1934	500	31 Dec. 1934	29,406
Sierra Leone	Brit.	26 Apr. 1931	651	31 Dec. 1933	1,800,000
Somali Coast	French	1 Jan. 1931	628	31 Dec. 1933	70,000
Somaliland	Brit.	Apr. 1931	68	31 Dec. 1933	347,385
Somaliland	Ital.	21 Apr. 1931	1,668	31 Dec. 1933	1,000,000
South-West Africa	S.A.M.	30 June 1935	31,800	31 Dec. 1934	266,930
Southern Rhodesia	Brit.	30 June 1935	54,000	30 June 1935	1,258,860
Spanish Guinea	Span.	31 Dec. 1930	1,539	31 Dec. 1933	120,000
Sudan	Ang.E.	1933	5,341	31 Dec. 1934	5,816,390
Swaziland	Brit.	31 Dec. 1934	2,830	31 Dec. 1934	126,560
Tanganyika	Br. M.	31 Dec. 1934	8,193	31 Dec. 1934	4,988,338
Tangier	Int. A.	1934	16,500	1934	60,000
Togoland	Br. M.	30 June 1934	43	30 June 1934	328,077
Togoland	Fr. M.	31 Dec. 1934	418	31 Dec. 1934	762,629
Tunis	French	31 Dec. 1933	180,000	31 Dec. 1933	2,500,000
Uganda	Brit.	31 Dec. 1934	1,959	31 Dec. 1934	3,640,636
Union of South Africa	Br. D.	30 June 1935	1,944,200	30 June 1935	8,600,300
Zanzibar	Brit.	1931	278	31 Dec. 1934	244,104
Total			3,957,618		144,879,105

95

POPULATION MOVEMENTS

SOURCES FOR TABLE II

Total Population. For Bechuanaland, Cape Verde Islands, Eritrea, Ethiopia, Liberia, Libya, Morocco (French), Northern Africa (Span.), Portuguese Guinea, Réunion, St. Thomé and Principe, Sierra Leone, Somali Coast (French), Somaliland (Ital.), Span. Guinea, and Tunis, see *Statistical Year-Book of the League of Nations 1934/35*, pp. 18–19. For Gambia, Nigeria, and Somaliland (Brit.), see *Statistical Abstract for the British Empire 1924 to 1933*, p. 3.

Algeria. Census 8 March 1931 (see Statistique générale de la France, *Résultats statistiques du recensement général de la population 1931*, vol. i, part i, p. 114): Municipal population, 881,584 Europeans (733,242 French, 109,821 Spaniards, 26,136 Italians, 3,706 Anglo-Maltese, 8,679 Others) and 5,588,314 Natives. There was besides the municipal population a population enumerated separately (troops, &c.), which at the 1931 census comprised 39,204 Europeans and 44,349 Natives (see *Statesman's Year-Book*, 1935, p. 911). For total population, June 1934, see League of Nations, Health Organisation, *Annual Epidemiological Report 1934*, p. 65. We have roughly estimated the number of Whites.

Angola. See *Boletim Trimestral da Repartição Central de Estatística Geral 1934*, p. 114. Military force 4,619 (419 Europeans, 4,200 Natives), see *Statesman's Year-Book*, 1935, p. 1240.

Basutoland. For Whites, see *South and East African Year Book and Guide*, 1936, p. 171; for total population, see *Annual Colonial Reports*, No. 1723, p. 5.

Bechuanaland. For Europeans, see *Annual Colonial Reports*, No. 1742, p. 6.

Belgian Congo. See *Congo*, 1936, vol. i, pp. 611–12. The figure 17,845 comprises all non-natives.

Cameroons (Brit. Mandate). See *Report to the Council of the League of Nations on the Administration of the Cameroons under British Mandate 1934*, pp. 110–11.

APPENDIX

Cameroons (French Mandate). Official evaluation 31 Dec. 1934 (see *Rapport annuel au Conseil de la Société des Nations sur l'administration sous mandat du territoire du Cameroun 1934*, pp. 120–2): 2,106 'Europeans' (1,619 French, 344 of other European nationalities, 83 Americans, 1 Canadian, 54 Libano-Syrians, 5 Armenians), and 2,228,095 'Natives'. The figure of 2,106 includes 531 officials and 421 wives and children of officials.

Cape Verde Islands. For Europeans, see population table in *Report on African Affairs 1933*, ed. by Owen Clough.

Egypt. Census 1927 (see *Population Census of Egypt 1927*, part i, pp. 192–201): 13,952,264 Egyptians, 225,600 foreigners (170 Africans, 1,636 Americans, 10,323 Asiatics, 213,471 Europeans). For total population 1934, see Royaume d'Égypte, *Annuaire Statistique 1932–1933*, p. 11. We have estimated roughly the number of Whites.

Eritrea. See *Annuario statistico italiano 1935*, p. 286.

Ethiopia. We have roughly estimated the number of Whites.

French Equatorial Africa. Census 1 July 1931 (see *Résultats statistiques du recensement 1931*, vol. i, part i, p. 113): 4,687 'Europeans and Assimilated'. They comprised 3,806 French, 785 persons with another specified European nationality, 22 Syrians, and 74 Others.

French West Africa. Official evaluation 31 Dec. 1934: 24,719 Europeans and Assimilated (17,631 French, 7,088 foreigners) and 14,432,021 Natives. In 1921 there were among 1,516 foreign Europeans and Assimilated in the Senegal Colony (1934: 5,157), 150 Europeans, 1,227 Syrians, 3 Chinese, 5 Hindus, and 131 Moroccans (see *Recensement de la population des colonies françaises 1921*, p. 15). We have assumed that in 1934 there were 1,000 Whites among the 7,088 foreign Europeans and Assimilated.

Gambia. Census 24 April 1931 (see *Report and Summary of the Census of the Gambia*, pp. 6–7): 274 'non-Africans' (226 with a

European nationality, 2 'Americans', 32 Syrians, 2 West Indians, 12 'Others'), and 199,246 Africans.

Gold Coast (comprising Gold Coast Colony, Colony of Ashanti, and Protectorate of Northern Colonies). Census 26 April 1931 (see *The Gold Coast 1931*, by A. W. Cardinall, Chief Census Officer, Appendices, p. 23): 3,035 resident non-Africans, of whom by nationality 2,367 were Europeans, 18 'Americans', 20 West Indians, and 630 Asiatics; there were, in addition, 72 Europeans and 32 Americans enumerated on ship-board. Resident Africans, 30 June 1934: 3,113,058 (see *Annual Colonial Reports*, No. 1748, p. 8).

Kenya. See *Annual Colonial Reports*, No. 1722, p. 12.

Liberia. For Whites, see *Statesman's Year-Book*, 1935, p. 1102.

Libya. See *Annuario statistico italiano 1935*, p. 286.

Madagascar (incl. dependencies). Official evaluation, 31 Dec. 1933: 26,454 'Europeans' (23,989 French, 2,465 foreigners), 1,654 Mulattos (1,198 French, 456 foreigners), and 3,792,879 non-Whites (3,781,638 French, 192 British, 941 Africans, 7,621 Hindus, 2,487 Chinese). The total of 3,820,987 includes 6,778 Army and Navy (1,831 Europeans, 4,947 non-Whites). A similar evaluation as of 31 Dec. 1932 (see *Bulletin de l'Agence Générale des Colonies 1934*, p. 549) included among 2,569 'European' foreigners 13 Asiatics.

Mauritius and dependencies. Census 26 April 1931 (see *Final Report on the Census Enumeration made in the Colony of Mauritius and its Dependencies*, p. 6): Mauritius, 645 Europeans (persons born in Europe of European parents or born in Mauritius of European parents). For total population, see *Annual Colonial Reports*, No. 1731, p. 7.

Morocco (French). Census 8 March 1931 (see *Résultats statistiques du recensement 1931*, vol. i, part i, p. 114): 172,481 non-Moroccan civilians (128,177 French, 22,684 Spaniards, 12,602 Italians, and 9,018 of other nationalities), 40,051 non-Moroccan military persons, and 5,192,000 Moroccans. We have roughly estimated the total number of white civilians.

APPENDIX

Morocco. (Spanish). See *Notiziario demografico*, 1935, p. 73.

Mozambique. See *Almanach de Gotha*, 1936, p. 1283. Military force 2,814 (572 Europeans, 2,242 Natives); see *Statesman's Year-Book*, 1935, p. 1242.

Nigeria. Census 23 April 1931 (see *Census of Nigeria*, vol. i, pp. 8, 32): incl. the Mandated Territories of British Cameroons, 4,952 Whites ('Europeans, Americans, and persons of European and American extraction, whatever their nationality') and 19,923,219 non-Whites. According to *Report on the Administration of the Cameroons under British Mandate 1931*, p. 88, there were in the British Cameroons in 1931, 278 Europeans.

Northern Africa (Span.). Census 31 Dec. 1930 (*Censo de la Población de España 1930*, vol. i, pp. 370–87, 406–7): 31,905 born in Northern Africa, 72,125 born in Spain, 8,436 born abroad (5,429 in Morocco, 620 in Algeria, 2 in Egypt, 5 in Turkey, &c.), 1,461 not stated. We have roughly estimated the number of Whites.

Northern Rhodesia. Census 5 May 1931 (see Northern Rhodesia, *Report of the Director of Census regarding the Census 1931*, pp. 7, 43): 13,486 Europeans, 176 Asiatics, 425 Mixed and Coloured, and 1,331,229 Natives. For 31 Dec. 1934 the Europeans and the Natives have been estimated at 11,464 and 1,366,425 respectively (see Northern Rhodesia, *Blue Book 1934*, Section 15, pp. 2–3).

Nyasaland. See *Annual Colonial Reports*, No. 1739, p. 6.

Portuguese Guinea. For Whites, see *Almanach de Gotha*, 1936, p. 1281. Military force 287 (23 Europeans, 264 Natives); see *Statesman's Year-Book*, 1935, p. 1240.

Réunion. Census 1 July 1931 (see *Résultats statistiques du recensement 1931*, vol. i, part i, p. 113): 192,961 'Europeans and Assimilated' and 4,972 Others (921 Malagasies, 302 Caffres, 1,311 Arabs, 196 Indians, 2,242 Chinese). According to the enumeration of 31 Dec. 1848, the last one to consider colour, the resident population consisted of 37,290 Whites and 66,201 Coloured (see *Tableaux de population*, &c., 1848, p. 19). We have assumed that the Whites constitute to-day 35 per cent. of the total population.

Rio de Oro (incl. Ifni). See *Statistical Year-Book of the League of Nations*.

Ruanda-Urundi (Belgian Mandate). See *Almanach de Gotha*, 1936, p. 828.

St. Helena and dependencies. Census 1931: in St. Helena, 3,851 'Islanders', 142 'Other British residents', and 2 'Other National'; in Ascension, 152 'St. Helenians', and 36 'Other British residents'. For 31 Dec. 1934, the total population of St. Helena has been estimated at 4,224, and of Ascension at 173 (114 St. Helenians and 59 Other British residents). See *Annual Colonial Reports*, No. 1736, p. 6. We have roughly estimated the number of Whites.

St. Thomé and Principe Islands. Census 1921 (see *Statesman's Year-Book*, 1935, p. 1240): 1,115 Whites, 57,123 Natives, 817 Others.

Seychelles. Census 26 April 1931 (see Colony of Seychelles, *Census for the Year 1931*, pp. 5–6): 26,706 Europeans, persons of European descent, and Africans (born in Europe, 147; in Asia, 8; in Africa, 26,546; in America, 4; in Australia, 1), 503 Indians, and 235 Chinese. For total population, see *The Seychelles Blue Book 1934*, p. 107. We have roughly estimated the number of Whites.

Sierra Leone. Census 26 April 1931 (see Sierra Leone, *Report of Census 1931*, pp. 63, 165): 651 Europeans out of a total population of 1,768,480. The latter figure includes the military population (of which 942 in military barracks; see ibid., pp. 20, 72), but not the population on board ships (67 Europeans, 84 Africans; see ibid., p. 73).

Somali Coast. Census 1 Jan. 1931: 1,362 Europeans and Assimilated (356 French, 9 English, 80 Italians, 4 Belgians, 130 Greeks, 49 of other European nationalities, 499 Indians, 157 Abyssinians, 78 Jews) and 68,420 Natives.

Somaliland (Brit.). For Europeans, see *Annual Colonial Reports*, No. 1707, p. 6.

APPENDIX

Somaliland (Ital.). See *Annuario statistico italiano 1935*, p. 286.

South-West Africa (South African Mandate). For Whites, see *Year Book of the Union of South Africa*, 1933–4, p. 996; for total population, see *Almanach de Gotha*, 1936, p. 1017.

Southern Rhodesia. See *Economic and Statistical Bulletin of Southern Rhodesia*, 20 Aug. 1935.

Spanish Guinea. Census 31 Dec. 1930 (*Anuario Estadístico de España*, 1934, p. 18): 1,539 Whites, 165,463 Natives.

Sudan. For Europeans, see *Report on African Affairs 1933*; for total population, see *Almanach de Gotha*, 1936, p. 974.

Swaziland (Brit.). See *Annual Colonial Reports*, No. 1740, p. 5.

Taganyika (Brit. Mandate). Estimate 31 Dec. 1934 (see Tanganyika Territory, *Blue Book 1934*, p. 121): 8,193 Europeans, 29,640 Asiatics, and 4,950,505 Natives.

Tangier. See *Statesman's Year-Book*, 1936, p. 1138.

Togoland (Brit. Mandate). See *Report to the Council of the League of Nations on the Administration of Togoland under British Mandate 1934*, p. 51.

Togoland (French Mandate). Evaluation 31 Dec. 1934 (see *Rapport annuel au Conseil de la Société des Nations sur l'administration sous mandat du territoire du Togo, 1934*, p. 81): 418 Europeans, 55 Libanians, and 762,156 Natives.

Tunis. Census 22 March 1931 (see *Résultats statistiques du recensement 1931*, vol. i, part i, p. 115): 195,293 'Europeans' (91,427 French, 91,178 Italians, 8,643 Maltese, 4,045 Other Europeans) and 2,215,399 'Natives'. The figures include only the civil population.

Uganda. See *Annual Colonial Reports*, No. 1729, p. 8; *Almanach de Gotha*, 1936, p. 952.

Union of South Africa. See *Year Book of the Union of South Africa*, 1933–4, p. 881.

Zanzibar. See *Annual Colonial Reports*, No. 1706, p. 6.

POPULATION MOVEMENTS

TABLE III. *White and Negro Population in America about 1835*

NORTH AMERICA

Countries	Date	White	Troops from Europe	Negro
United States . .	31 Dec. 1835	12,445,000	—	2,619,000
Canada (Brit.) . .	31 Dec. 1835	1,300,000	4,053	5,000
Newfoundland (Brit.) .	1836	73,705	..	—
Greenland (Dan.) .	1840	251	..	—
St. Pierre and Miquelon (French) .	31 Dec. 1835	1,472	11	—
Alaska (Russian) .	1830	940	..	—
Total		13,821,368	4,064	2,624,000

CENTRAL AMERICA

Mexico . . .	1827	1,200,000	—	50,000
Republic of Central America . .	1835	50,000	—	25,000
Haiti . .	1827	20,000	—	910,000
British Honduras .	31 Dec. 1835	222	743	2,321
British West Indies:				
Jamaica . .	1835	15,000	2,881	370,000
Cayman Islands .	1827	100	—	1,500
Trinidad . .	1834	3,632	350	39,381
Tobago . .	1833	304	100	12,894
Grenada . .	1834	661	200	24,761
St. Vincent . .	1835	1,300	250	26,000
Barbados . .	1834	12,797	500	89,434
St. Lucia . .	1835	881	300	13,669
Dominica . .	1833	720	250	18,000
St. Kitts . .	1834	1,200	50	22,280
Montserrat . .	1834	312	50	7,228
Antigua . .	1834	1,900	200	33,016
Barbuda . .	..	50	—	1,450
Nevis . . .	1831	700	50	11,142
Anguilla . .	..	200	—	1,800
Tortola and Virgin Islands . .	1834	800	50	5,735

APPENDIX

CENTRAL AMERICA (*cont.*)

Countries	Date	White	Troops from Europe	Negro
Bahamas (Brit.) .	1834	4,667	200	13,195
Bermudas (Brit.) .	1835	4,264	600	4,456
St. Croix (Dan.) .	31 Dec. 1825	2,223	..	30,128
St. Jean (Dan.) .	31 Dec. 1825	150	..	5,040
St. Thomas (Dan.) .	31 Dec. 1825	850	..	2,926
Curaçao (Dutch) .	1830	2,781	..	10,059
St. Eustache (Dutch) .	1830	1,000	..	15,000
St. Martin (Dutch) .	1830	500	..	5,500
Guadeloupe (French)	31 Dec. 1835	12,000	2,138	116,000
Martinique (French) .	31 Dec. 1835	9,500	2,020	107,000
Cuba (Span.) . .	31 Dec. 1835	370,000	..	520,000
Puerto Rico (Span.) .	1836	188,869	..	168,217
St. Barthélemy (Swed.)	1827	1,992	..	6,210
Total		1,909,575	10,932	2,669,342

SOUTH AMERICA

	Date	White	Troops from Europe	Negro
Argentine . .	31 Dec. 1835	600,000	—	50,000
Brazil . . .	31 Dec. 1835	1,100,000	—	3,700,000
Other Independent States . .	31 Dec. 1835	1,200,000	—	550,000
Guiana (Brit.) . .	1834	2,883	700	91,060
Falkland Isl. and dep. (Brit.) . .	..	25	..	—
Surinam (Dutch) .	1830	2,029	..	55,012
Guiana (French) .	31 Dec. 1836	1,273	623	20,665
Total		2,906,210	1,323	4,466,737

AMERICA

		White	Troops from Europe	Negro
Total		18,637,153	16,319	9,760,079

The sign '—' indicates nil, the sign '..' unknown.

SOURCES FOR TABLE III

United States. The number of Whites was 10,537,378 on 1 June 1830, and 14,195,805 on 1 June 1840, the number of Negroes 2,328,642 and 2,873,648 (see Bureau of the Census, *A Century of Population Growth*, p. 80, Washington, 1909). We have assumed that both Whites and Negroes increased in geometrical progression.

Canada. Martin (*Statistics*, 'Chart') gives 1,335,400 Whites. To judge from the details given in *Statistics of Canada*, vol. iv, *Censuses of Canada 1665 to 1871*, his total for Whites, owing to an over-estimate for Upper Canada, is somewhat too high. For troops, see *Parliamentary Papers 1837-8*, vol. 37, pp. 134-5. We have roughly estimated the number of Negroes.

Newfoundland. See *Censuses of Canada 1665 to 1871*, p. xlviii.

Greenland. See Danmarks Statistik, *Population du Groënland 1930*, p. 33, Copenhagen, 1932.

St. Pierre and Miquelon. See *Annales maritimes et coloniales 1837*, part ii, vol. i, p. 1160; *Notices statistiques*, vol. iv (1840), p. 99. We have included among the civil residents the 989 fixed inhabitants (*habitants sédentaires*) and the 450 wintering fishers (*pêcheurs hivernants*), but not the 1,370 fishers and mariners (*passagers et marins*) who had come from France for the fishing season (see *Notices statistiques*, vol. iv, pp. 93, 128); the civilians include also 33 officials. The figures for officials and troops refer to 1840.

Alaska. According to Malte-Brun, *Abrégé de géographie*, 2nd ed., p. 809, Paris, 1838, 910 in Alaska and about 30 in Bodega.

Mexico. For Whites, see 'Statistische Übersicht von America für 1827', *Neue Allgemeine Geographische und Statistische Ephemeriden*, vol. 23, Weimar, 1827. We have roughly estimated the number of Negroes.

Republic of Central America. 'Statistische Übersicht von America für 1827' gives 180,000 Whites, 952,400 Indians and Free Coloured, and 5,000 Negro and Mulatto slaves. G. A. Thompson (*Narrative of an Official Visit to Guatemala from*

APPENDIX

Mexico, p. 452, London, 1829) says that of the total population of 2,000,000 the Whites and Creoles constitute one-fifth, and the Mixed Classes and the Indians two-fifths each, but adds: 'Of Europeans, or perfect whites, there are not more than 5,000.'

Haiti. 'Statistische Übersicht von America für 1827' gives 20,000 Whites and 915,335 Indians and Free Coloured.

British Honduras. See *Archives of British Honduras*, vol. ii, pp. 343, 382, London, 1934. Troops refer to 31 Dec. 1832; they include 492 Military Pensioners.

British West Indies. Sources, if not otherwise stated: Martin, *Statistics*; Martin, *The British Colonies*, vol. iv, part ii.

Jamaica. The statements are quite contradictory. Moreau de Jonnès, p. 43, gives for 1832: 15,000 Whites, 68,334 Free Coloured, and 302,666 slaves. Martin, *Statistics* (1839), p. 8, gives 35,000 Whites, 1,200 Maroons, 70,000 Free Coloured, and 310,368 slaves; according to a general census of 1844 quoted in his *British Colonies*, vol. iv, part ii, p. 94, there were 15,776 Whites and 361,657 Coloured. For troops, see Martin, *Statistics*, Appendix, p. 17.

St. Vincent. The number of Whites was 1,301 in 1825 and 1,268 in 1844; the number of Coloured was 26,604 in 1825 and 25,980 in 1844. See Martin, *Statistics*, p. 54, and 'Chart'; *British Colonies*, vol. iv, part ii, p. 129.

St. Lucia. See *Parliamentary Papers 1837–8*, vol. 47, p. 469; Martin, *Statistics*, 'Chart'.

Nevis. See *Parliamentary Papers 1835*, vol. 49, p. 761; Martin, *Statistics*, 'Chart'.

Bahamas. See *Parliamentary Papers 1837*, vol. 49, p. 544; Martin, *Statistics*, 'Chart'.

Bermudas. See *Parliamentary Papers 1837–8*, vol. 47, p. 484; Martin, *Statistics*, 'Chart'.

St. Croix, St. Jean, St. Thomas. See *Geographische und Statistische Ephemeriden*, vol. 21, Weimar, 1827, pp. 351–2.

Curaçao, St. Eustache, St. Martin. See Moreau de Jonnès, pp. 49–50.

POPULATION MOVEMENTS

Guadeloupe. The number of Whites was 11,569 in 1826 (see Moreau de Jonnès, p. 19). Their number does not seem to have been ascertained at any later census. The ministry of the navy and the colonies estimates their number at 11,000 or 12,000 for 31 Dec. 1835 (see *Notices statistiques*, vol. i, p. 163). The figures for officials (441) and troops (2,138) refer to 1836. The total (white and black) resident population on 31 Dec. 1835 was 127,574 (see ibid., p. 163).

Martinique. The number of Whites was 9,362 in 1830 (see *Tableaux de population*, &c., 1843, p. 14), and 10,105 on 31 Dec. 1839 (see ibid., 1839, p. 16). The ministry of the navy and the colonies estimated it at about 9,000 for 31 Dec. 1835 (see *Notices statistiques*, vol. i, p. 49). The figures for officials (519) and troops (2,010) refer to 1836. The total (white and black) resident population on 31 Dec. 1835 was 116,031 (see ibid., p. 49).

Cuba. Census 31 Dec. 1827 (see *Cuadro estadístico de la Isla de Cuba 1827*, p. 26, Habana, 1829): 311,051 Whites, 106,494 Free Coloured, 286,942 slaves. Census 1841 (see *Report on the Census of Cuba, 1899*, p. 710, Washington, 1900): 418,291 Whites, 152,838 Free Coloured, 436,495 slaves. We have roughly estimated the number of Whites and Negroes for 31 Dec. 1835.

Puerto Rico. See *Parliamentary Papers 1839*, vol. 45, p. 324.

St. Barthélemy. See 'Statistische Übersicht von America für 1827'.

Argentine. Sir Woodbine Parish (*Buenos Ayres and the Provinces of the Rio de La Plata*, p. 393, London, 1838) gives for 1836–7 as total population excl. Indians 600,000–675,000. 'Statistische Übersicht von America für 1827' gives 600,000 Whites, 1,400,000 Indians and Free Coloured, and 25,000 Negro and Mulatto slaves. We have assumed that in 1835 there were altogether 50,000 Negroes (incl. Mulattos).

Brazil. The statements are most contradictory. The introduction to the census report for 1920 (*Recenseamento do Brazil 1920*, vol. i, Rio de Janeiro, 1922), on the authority of Rugendas, gives (p. 334) for 1835, 845,000 Whites, 628,000 Mestizos, and 1,987,000 Negroes. Rugendas (a German painter who in 1821, at the age of 19 years, went to Brazil and returned to Europe in 1825) actually gives in his *Voyage pittoresque dans le Brésil*, section ii, p. 1, Paris, 1835: 843,000 Whites, 628,000 'Coloured', 1,987,500 Negroes, and 300,000 Indians; but he does not mention the date to which his figures refer, and they evidently refer to the end of 1818, for which date Balbi ('Essai statistique sur le Nouveau Monde', *Scritti geografici*, &c., vol. iii, p. 251) gives 843,000 Whites, 426,000 Free Mulattos, Mestizos, and Negro-Indians, 202,000 Mulatto slaves, 159,500 Free Negroes, 1,728,000 Negro slaves, and 259,400 subdued Indians, and at the same time states that children under 7 and unsubdued Indians are not included. 'Statistische Übersicht von America für 1827' gives 900,000 Whites, 1,250,000 Indians and Free Coloured, and 3,156,418 Negro and Mulatto slaves. Malte-Brun (according to the census report for 1920, vol. i, pp. 406–7) estimates for 1830: 1,347,000 Whites, 1,748,000 Coloured, 2,017,000 Negroes, and 228,000 Indians. In making our own estimate we have started from these figures for 1830, have assumed that 20 per cent. or 270,000 of the persons counted as Whites were actually Mulattos or Mestizos, that 75 per cent. of the 1,748,000 + 270,000 Coloured were Mulattos, and that the Mulattos and (owing to large slave imports) also the Negroes increased until 1836 somewhat more than the Whites.

Other Independent States in South America. 'Statistische Übersicht von America für 1827' gives the following figures:

Country	White, Europeans, Creoles	Indians and Free Coloured	Negro and Mulatto Slaves
Bolivia	250,000	755,000	5,000
Chile	110,000	452,000	40,000
Colombia	700,000	1,936,000	130,397
Paraguay	60,000	540,000	..
Peru	140,000	1,373,839	50,000
Total	1,260,000	5,056,839	225,397

All these figures are quite uncertain. Taking into account estimates of other authorities, we have entered for 31 Dec. 1835: 1,200,000 Whites and 550,000 Negroes (including Mulattos).

British Guiana, Falkland Islands. See Martin, *Statistics*, 'Chart'; Martin, *British Colonies*, vol. iv, part ii, p. 179.

Surinam. See Moreau de Jonnès, pp. 49–50.

French Guiana. The number of Whites was 1,280 in 1827 (see Moreau de Jonnès, p. 22), and 1,025 on 31 Dec. 1838 (see *Notices statistiques*, vol. iv, p. 158). The ministry of the navy and the colonies estimated their number for 31 Dec. 1836 at about 1,100 (see ibid., vol. ii, p. 178). For officials (173) and troops (623), see ibid., p. 183 (we presume that these are the figures for Whites only). The total (white and black) population (incl. all officials and troops) on 31 Dec. 1836 was 22,661 (see ibid., pp. 182–3).

APPENDIX

TABLE IV. *Races in America about 1935*

NORTH AMERICA

Countries	Date	White	Indian	Negro	Other	Total
Alaska (U.S.)	1 Oct. 1929	28,640	30,012	136	490	59,278
Canada (Br. D.)	1 June 1934	10,591,000	129,000	20,000	95,000	10,835,000
Greenland (Dan.)	1 Oct. 1930	408	..	..	16,222	16,630
Labrador (Newf.)	31 Dec. 1934	3,151	..	..	1,300	4,451
Newfoundland (Br. D.)	31 Dec. 1934	289,272	200	..	..	289,472
St. Pierre and Miquelon (Fr.)	1 July 1931	4,321	..	..	..	4,321
United States	30 June 1935	112,763,000	1,818,000	12,317,000	274,000	127,172,000
Total		123,679,792	1,977,212	12,337,136	387,012	138,381,152

CENTRAL AMERICA

Countries	Date	White	Indian	Negro	Other	Total
Antigua (Br.)	31 Dec. 1934	1,015	..	32,045	..	33,060
Bahamas (Br.)	31 Dec. 1934	10,202	..	53,561	..	63,763
Barbados (Br.)	31 Dec. 1934	12,771	..	169,669	..	182,440
Bermuda (Br.)	31 Dec. 1934	11,807	..	17,848	..	29,655
Brit. Honduras (Br.)	31 Dec. 1934	1,095	53,102	..	547	54,744
Cayman Islands (Br.)	Aug. 1934	2,368	2	3,637	2	6,009
Costa Rica	31 Dec. 1934	480,613	56,543	28,271	..	565,427
Cuba	31 Dec. 1934	2,711,949	..	1,252,282	23,929	3,988,160
Curaçao (Dutch)	31 Dec. 1934	3,330	..	79,091	833	83,254
Dominica (Br.)	31 Dec. 1934	695	420	45,183	..	46,298
Dominican Rep.	May 1935	59,125	7,391	1,404,214	7,391	1,478,121
Grenada (Br.)	31 Dec. 1934	1,031	..	79,451	3,406	83,888
Guadeloupe (Fr.)	31 Dec. 1933	21,600	..	248,400	..	270,000
Guatemala	31 Dec. 1934	113,334	2,153,348	..	..	2,266,682
Haiti	31 Dec. 1934	10,000	..	2,490,000	..	2,500,000
Honduras	30 Nov. 1934	19,254	895,297	48,134	..	962,685
Jamaica (Br.)	31 Dec. 1934	18,718	..	1,057,215	28,842	1,104,775
Martinique (Fr.)	31 Dec. 1934	10,286	..	219,193	15,429	244,908
Mexico	31 Dec. 1933	1,700,000	15,840,000	10,000	50,000	17,600,000
Montserrat (Br.)	31 Dec. 1934	105	..	13,056	..	13,161
Nicaragua	31 Dec. 1933	134,400	588,800	76,800	..	800,000
Panama	31 Dec. 1933	81,565	302,692	95,241	4,282	483,780
Panama Canal Zone (U.S.)	30 June 1934	22,120	..	23,970	310	46,400
Puerto Rico (U.S.)	30 June 1935	1,239,550	2	429,310	38	1,668,900
St. Kitts and Nevis (Br.)	31 Dec. 1934	1,197	..	36,324	..	37,521
St. Lucia (Br.)	31 Dec. 1934	1,000	..	62,804	..	63,804
St. Vincent (Br.)	31 Dec. 1934	2,429	..	49,808	1,385	53,622
Salvador	31 Dec. 1934	78,725	1,495,770	..	..	1,574,495
Trinidad & Tobago (Br.)	31 Dec. 1934	43,206	..	237,632	151,220	432,058
Turks & Caicos Is. (Br.)	31 Dec. 1934	160	..	5,140	..	5,300
Virgin Is. (Br.)	31 Dec. 1934	38	..	5,450	..	5,488
Virgin Is. (U.S.)	1 Apr. 1930	2,010	..	19,962	40	22,012
Total		6,795,698	21,393,367	8,293,691	287,654	36,770,410

TABLE IV (*cont.*)

SOUTH AMERICA

Countries	Date	White	Indian	Negro	Other	Total
Argentine	31 Dec. 1934	11,914,000	100,000	50,000	100,000	12,164,000
Bolivia	31 Dec. 1933	450,000	2,490,000	57,000	3,000	3,000,000
Brazil	31 Dec. 1933	18,409,000	10,327,000	15,939,500	224,500	44,900,000
Brit. Guiana (Br.)	31 Dec. 1934	2,039	8,601	173,125	139,406	323,171
Chile	31 Dec. 1935	3,177,000	1,299,000	20,000	10,000	4,506,000
Colombia	30 June 1934	2,928,989	5,145,021	284,530	10,000	8,368,540
Ecuador	31 Dec. 1933	160,000	1,560,000	280,000	..	2,000,000
Falkland Is. and dep. (Br.)	31 Dec. 1934	3,087	..	..	..	3,087
French Guiana, Inini (Fr.)	31 Dec. 1933	25,000	1,000	..	..	26,000
Paraguay	31 Dec. 1933	90,000	800,000	10,000	..	900,000
Peru	1934	625,000	5,325,000	200,000	100,000	6,250,000
Surinam (Dutch)	31 Dec. 1934	1,886	66,682	17,000	78,517	164,085
Uruguay	31 Dec. 1934	2,017,040	1,000	1,000	1,000	2,020,040
Venezuela	31 Dec. 1933	99,000	2,046,000	1,155,000	..	3,300,000
Total		39,902,041	29,169,304	18,187,155	666,423	87,924,923

AMERICA

Total		170,377,531	52,539,883	38,817,982	1,341,089	263,076,485

SOURCES FOR TABLE IV

Where no source is mentioned we have applied the proportions given by Loyo to the most recent population estimate in *Statistical Year-Book of the League of Nations 1934/35*, pp. 19–20 (for Bahamas to the population in *Annual Colonial Reports*, No. 1738, p. 6; for Cuba to the population in Department of Overseas Trade, *Economic Conditions in Cuba*, April 1935, p. 18; for Martinique to the population in *Revue d'histoire des colonies*, 1935, p. 146; for Chile to the population in *Estadística Chilena*, 1935, No. 12; for Peru and Colombia to the population in *Boletín de la Oficina Sanitaria Panamericana*, 1935, p. 279, 1936, p. 187). In a few cases, where Loyo does not take account of the small numbers of Negroes or 'Others' (Chile, Colombia, Paraguay), we have slightly revised his percentages. For Canada, United States, Antigua, Grenada, Jamaica, Panama, Panama Canal Zone, Puerto Rico, St. Kitts and Nevis, and

APPENDIX

St. Vincent, we have assumed that the proportions of the races have remained the same since the last census.

Alaska. Census 1 Oct. 1929 (see *Census of the United States 1930, Outlying Territories and Possessions*, pp. 13, 15): 28,640 Whites, 29,983 Indians (full-blooded and of mixed Indian and other blood), 26 Chinese, 278 Japanese, 136 Negroes, 164 Filipinos, 29 Mexicans, 11 Hawaiians, 11 Koreans. Total population, 30 June 1935: 61,500 (see *Statistical Abstract of the United States 1935*, p. 10).

Canada. Census 1 June 1931 (see *Census of Canada 1931*, vol. ii, pp. 294–7): 10,134,313 European races, 46,519 Chinese, 23,342 Japanese, 14,687 Other Asiatic races, 5,979 Eskimoes, 122,911 Indians, 19,456 Negroes, 681 Various, 8,898 Unspecified. Total population, 1 June 1934, see *Canada Year Book 1934–35*, p. 164.

Greenland. Census 1 Oct. 1930 (see Danmarks Statistik, *Population du Groënland 1930*, p. 5): 408 Europeans, 16,222 Natives.

Labrador. Total population, see *Statesman's Year-Book*, 1936, p. 348. 'Some 1,300 Eskimo, the remainder of British descent' (*The Dominions Office and Colonial Office List 1935*, p. 134).

Newfoundland. Total population, see *Statesman's Year-Book*, 1936, p. 348. We have roughly estimated the number of Indians.

St. Pierre and Miquelon. Census 1 July 1931 (see *Résultats statistiques du recensement 1931*, vol. i, part i, p. 113): 4,321 Europeans and Assimilated (4,067 French, 254 foreigners).

United States of America. Census 1 April 1930 (see *Census of the United States 1930, Population*, vol. ii, p. 25): 108,864,207 Whites, 11,891,143 Negroes, 1,422,533 Mexicans, 332,397 Indians, 74,954 Chinese, 138,834 Japanese, 45,208 Filipinos, 3,130 Hindus, 1,860 Koreans, 660 Hawaiians, 96 Malays, 18 Siamese, 6 Samoans. Total population, 30 June 1935, see *Statistical Abstract of the United States 1935*, p. 10.

Antigua. Census 24 April 1921: 914 White, 3,999 Coloured,

24,854 Black; total population, 31 Dec. 1934: 33,060 (see *Annual Colonial Reports*, No. 1734, p. 5).

Barbados. *Annual Colonial Reports*, No. 1725, p. 6, states: 'Based on the returns given in the last census (1921) the population is made up as follows: White 7 per cent, Black 71 per cent, Mixed 22 per cent.' We have applied these percentages to the total population shown ibid., p. 5.

Bermuda. Civil population 31 Dec. 1934 (see Bermuda, *Report of the Registrar General 1934*, p. 2): 11,807 White, 17,848 Coloured. In addition: Military 526, their families 181, Naval employees, &c. (census 17 May 1931), 666.

British Honduras. Total population, see *Annual Colonial Reports*, No. 1713, p. 6. 'The total number of residents of unblemished white stock is certainly not in excess of 200, men, women and children' (*South American Handbook 1936*, p. 218). According to *Almanach de Gotha*, 1936, p. 965, in 1934 about 600 Europeans, 200 North Americans, and 2,000 Creoles. We have allocated 2 per cent. to White, 97 per cent. to Indian, and 1 per cent. to 'Other' (Syrian, Chinese).

Cayman Islands. See *Annual Colonial Reports*, No. 1745, p. 8.

Costa Rica. Total population, see *Statesman's Year-Book*, 1936, p. 793. According to Loyo: 90 per cent. Whites, 3 per cent. Indians, 3 per cent. Mestizos, 2 per cent. Negroes, 2 per cent. Mulattos. According to *Almanach de Gotha*, 1936, p. 870: 85 per cent. Whites, 2 per cent. Indians, 10 per cent. Mixed, 3 per cent. Negroes from the British West Indies. We have allocated 85 per cent. to Whites, 10 per cent. to Indians, and 5 per cent. to Negroes.

Curaçao. According to Huebner's *Geographisch-statistische Tabellen 1929*, p. 250, in 1926: 55,000 Black, 1,200 Europeans, 1,600 Other foreigners. Loyo counts 7·2 per cent. for White and 92·8 for Negro. Total population, 31 Dec. 1934, see *Statistical Annual of Curaçao*, 1934, p. 3. We have allocated 4 per cent. to White, 95 per cent. to Negro, and 1 per cent. to Others.

Dominica. Census 24 April 1921 (see Dominica *Census 1921*,

p. vi): 556 Whites, 11,563 Coloured, 24,940 Black. The Caribs (according to *Almanach de Gotha*, 1936, p. 967, 420 in 1930) were grouped with 'Coloured' (see *Census 1921*, p. vii). Total population, 31 Dec. 1934, see *Annual Colonial Reports*, No. 1734, p. 5. We have assumed that the proportions of the races have remained the same, but have segregated 420 for Indians.

Dominican Republic. Census 24 Dec. 1920 (see Huebner's *Tabellen 1929*, p. 204): 223,000 White, 445,000 Mixed, 227,000 Negro. Loyo counts 4 per cent. each for White and Negro, and 92 per cent. for Mulatto. Total population, see *South American Handbook 1936*, p. 38. We have allocated 4 per cent. to White, 0·5 per cent. to Indian, 95 per cent. to Negro, and 0·5 per cent. to Other (Syrians, &c.).

Grenada. Census 24 April 1921 (Grenada, *Report and General Abstracts of the Census of 1921*, p. 10): 905 White, 11,673 Mixed, 51,032 Black, 2,692 Oriental; but 'the "Whites" may safely be reduced by about 10 per cent. and the "Mixed" correspondingly increased'. Total population, 31 Dec. 1934, see *Annual Colonial Reports*, No. 1718, p. 5.

Guatemala. Total population, see *Boletín de la Oficina Sanitaria Panamericana*, 1936, p. 189. Loyo counts 10 per cent. for Whites, 60 per cent. for Indians, and 30 per cent. for Mestizos. Loyo evidently over-estimates the proportion of Whites. We have allocated 5 per cent. to Whites and 95 per cent. to Indians.

Haiti. Total population, see *Annual Epidemiological Report 1934*, p. 65. We have roughly estimated the number of Whites.

Honduras. Total population, see *Statesman's Year-Book*, 1936, p. 1018. Loyo counts 5 per cent. for Whites, 20 per cent. for Indians, 70 per cent. for Mestizos, and 5 per cent. for Negroes. According to *Almanach de Gotha*, 1936, p. 1143: 1·3 per cent. Creoles and Europeans, 10 per cent. Indians, 85·2 per cent. Mixed (Ladinos), and 2·4 per cent. Negroes. We have allocated 2 per cent. to Whites, 93 per cent. to Indians, and 5 per cent. to Negroes.

Jamaica. Census 25 April 1921 (see *Census of Jamaica and its Dependencies 1921*, p. 7): 14,476 White, 157,223 Coloured, 660,420 Black, 18,610 East Indian, 3,696 Chinese, 3,693 not stated. Total population, 31 Dec. 1934, see *Annual Colonial Reports*, No. 1730, p. 5.

Mexico. Census 30 Nov. 1921 (see *Resumen del Censo General 1921*, p. 62, Mexico, 1928): Mexican nationality: 4,179,449 Natives, 8,504,561 Mixed, 1,404,718 Whites, 144,094 Other races and unknown; Foreigners: 101,958. Census 15 May 1930 (see Dirección General de Estadística, *México en Cifras 1934*, pp. 16–17): 16,392,846 Mexicans and 159,876 Foreigners. The race was not ascertained at this census; *Statesman's Year-Book*, 1935, p. 1117, gives: 4,620,880 Indians, 9,040,590 Mixed, 2,444,466 Pure White, 140,094 Unknown, 159,876 Foreigners; Loyo counts 15 per cent. White, 30 per cent. Indian, 55 per cent. Mestizo; *South American Handbook 1936*, p. 387, counts 10 per cent. of pure white race, 30 per cent. of pure native blood, and 60 per cent. of mixed race. We have assumed that 90 per cent. of the total of 17,600,000 given for 31 Dec. 1933 in *Statistical Year-Book of the League of Nations* were Indians (incl. Mestizos), and that the remainder with the exception of 10,000 Negroes (incl. Mulattos) and 50,000 'Others' were White.

Montserrat. See Leeward Islands, *Blue Book 1934*, Section 15, p. 5.

Panama. Census 1930 (see *Notiziario Demografico*, 1935, p. 72): 78,813 Whites, 69,583 Negroes, 42,897 Indians, 4,138 Orientals, 249,583 Mestizos, 22,445 Mulattos. Total population, 31 Dec. 1933, see *Almanach de Gotha*, 1936, p. 1237.

Panama Canal Zone. Census 1 April 1930 (see *Census of the United States 1930, Outlying Territories*, &c., p. 328): 18,814 Whites, 20,385 Negroes, 34 Indians, 88 Chinese, 85 Hindus, 37 Filipinos, 24 Other Coloured. Total population, 30 June 1934, see *Statistical Abstract of the United States 1934*, p. 10.

Puerto Rico. Census 1 April 1930 (see *Census of the United*

States 1930, Outlying Territories, &c., pp. 133, 136): 1,146,719 Whites, 397,156 Coloured (Negroes and persons of mixed White and Negro blood), 2 Mexicans, 5 Indians, 23 Chinese, 6 Japanese, 2 Filipinos. Total population, 30 June 1935, see *Statistical Abstract of the United States 1935,* p. 10.

St. Kitts and Nevis. Census 24 April 1921: 1,219 White, 6,204 Coloured, 30,791 Black; total population 31 Dec. 1934: 37,521 (see *Annual Colonial Reports,* No. 1734, p. 5).

St. Lucia. Total population, see Saint Lucia, *Blue Book 1934,* p. 168. We have roughly estimated the number of Whites.

St. Vincent. Census 26 April 1931: 2,173 Whites, 11,292 Coloured, 33,257 Negroes, 1,239 Others; total population, 31 Dec. 1934: 53,622 (see *Colonial Annual Reports,* No. 1714, p. 4).

Salvador. See *Boletín de la Oficina Sanitaria Panamericana,* 1935, p. 899; *Almanach de Gotha,* 1936, p. 1300.

Trinidad and Tobago. Census 26 April 1931 (see *Annual Colonial Reports,* No. 1720, p. 7): Born in Europe, 1,891; North America, 614; South America, 5,082; China or locally born of Chinese parentage, 5,208; India or locally born of East Indian parentage, 137,583; Locally born, incl. those of European parentage and people of African and Mixed descent, 216,138; other West Indian Colonies and elsewhere, 46,267. Loyo counts 10 per cent. for Whites, 25 per cent. for Indians, 6 per cent. for Negroes, and 59 per cent. for Others. Total population, 31 Dec. 1934: 432,058 (see *Reports,* No. 1720, p. 7); we have assumed that of this population 10 per cent. were Whites, 55 per cent. Negroes (incl. Mulattos), and 35 per cent. Others.

Turks and Caicos Islands. See *Annual Colonial Reports,* No. 1733, p. 4.

Virgin Islands (Brit.). Census 24 April 1921: 36 White, 1,158 Coloured, 3,888 Black; total population, 31 Dec. 1934: 5,488 (see *Annual Colonial Reports,* No. 1734, p. 5).

Virgin Islands (U.S.A.). Census 1 April 1930 (see *Census of the United States 1930, Outlying Territories,* &c., pp. 261, 264):

2,010 White, 2,719 Mixed (White and Negro blood), 17,243 Negro, 4 Filipino, 1 Indian, 17 Chinese, 18 Hindu.

Argentine. No census since 1914. Total population, 31 Dec. 1934, see *Statistical Year-Book of the League of Nations*. We have roughly estimated the small numbers of non-Whites.

Bolivia. No census since 1900. An estimate of 1929 showed 426,212 White, 1,586,649 Indian, and 898,429 Mixed (see *Statesman's Year-Book*, 1935, p. 716). Loyo counts 15 per cent. Whites, 50 per cent. Indians, 33 per cent. Mestizos, and 2 per cent. Negroes. We have applied these proportions (counting 1·9 per cent. for Negroes and 0·1 per cent. for Others) to the estimated population of 31 Dec. 1933 given in *Statistical Year-Book of the League of Nations*.

Brazil. Census 31 Dec. 1890 (see *Sexo, raça*, &c., *da População Recenseada 1890*, pp. 2–3): 6,302,198 Whites, 2,097,426 Negroes, 1,295,796 Indians, 4,638,495 Mixed. The National Museum in 1922 counted 51 per cent. White, 2 per cent. Indian, 11 per cent. Mestizo, 14 per cent. Negro, and 22 per cent. Mulatto (see *Year Book of Brazil 1932*, p. 62); Loyo counts 41·0 per cent. White, 10·1 per cent. Indian, 33·3 per cent. Mestizo, 7·8 per cent. Negro, and 7·8 per cent. Mulatto. Total population, 31 Dec. 1933, see *Statistical Year-Book of the League of Nations*. We have allocated 41 per cent. to Whites, 23 per cent. to Indians, 35·5 per cent. to Negroes, and 0·5 per cent. to Others.

British Guiana. Registrar-General's estimate for 31 Dec. 1934 (see *Annual Colonial Reports*, No. 1728, p. 7): 2,039 Europeans other than Portuguese, 8,546 Portuguese, 136,004 East Indians, 3,099 Chinese, 8,601 Aborigines, 127,301 Blacks, 37,278 Mixed, 303 Other races and races not stated. We have assumed that the 'Portuguese' and the 'Mixed' were Mulattos.

Falkland Islands. See *Statistical Abstract for the British Empire 1924 to 1933*, p. 4; *Annual Colonial Reports*, No. 1699, p. 5; ibid., No. 1749, p. 5.

French Guiana and Inini Territory. Census 1 July 1931

(*Résultats statistiques du recensement général 1931*, vol. i, part i, p. 113): 28,310 Europeans and Assimilated (incl. 5,419 convicts), 1,000 Natives. Total population, 31 Dec. 1933, see *Statistical Year-Book of the League of Nations*.

Surinam. According to *Statistical Annual of Surinam*, 1934, pp. 3–4: 1,886 Europeans, 63,982 Natives, 33,560 Netherlands-Indians, 39,393 British East Indians, 2,014 Chinese, 17,000 Bush-negroes, 2,700 Aboriginal Indians, 3,550 Others.

Uruguay. Total population, see *Síntesis Estadística de la República Oriental del Uruguay*, Aug. 1935, p. 2. We have roughly estimated the race distribution.

TABLE V. *Races in Oceania about 1935*

Countries	Date	Whites	Natives	Others	Total
Australia	30 June 1935	6,674,456	80,609	29,240	6,784,305
New Zealand	31 Dec. 1935	1,485,984	75,934	6,302	1,568,220
Norfolk (Austral.)	30 June 1933	1,230	1	..	1,231
Papua (Austral.)	30 June 1933	1,148	274,755	813	276,716
Fiji Islands (Brit.)	31 Dec. 1934	4,763	106,560	86,126	197,449
Gilbert and Ellice (Brit.)	31 Dec. 1934	280	34,259	357	34,896
Brit. Solomon Islands (Brit.)	Apr. 1931	478	93,415	173	94,066
Tonga (Brit.)	Apr. 1934	378	30,957	254	31,589
Guam (U.S.)	1 Apr. 1930	1,205	16,402	902	18,509
Hawaii (U.S.)	1 Apr. 1930	80,373	50,860	237,103	368,336
American Samoa (U.S.)	1 Apr. 1930	227	9,803	25	10,055
French Settlements (Fr.)	1 July 1931	5,750	29,667	4,862	40,279
New Caledonia and dep. (Fr.)	1 July 1931	17,250	29,000	12,000	58,250
New Hebrides (Anglo-Fr.)	3¹ Dec. 1933	1,019	50,000	1,299	52,318
Cook Island (N.Z.)	30 Sept. 1935	313	16,072	..	16,385
Tokelau Islands (N.Z.)	Aug. 1935	..	1,198	..	1,198
New Guinea (Austr. M.)	30 June 1935	4,018	678,686	1,670	684,374
Nauru (Brit. M.)	1 Apr. 1935	158	1,603	935	2,696
Caroline, Marianne, and Marshall Islands (Jap. M.)	31 Dec. 1934	103	50,174	35,328	85,605
Western Samoa (N.Z.)	30 June 1935	623	52,570	597	53,790
Total		8,279,756	1,682,525	417,986	10,380,267

SOURCES FOR TABLE V

Australia. Census 30 June 1933 (see *Census of the Commonwealth of Australia 1933*, Bulletin No. 15, p. 8): 6,579,990 full-blood Europeans, 22,818 full-blood non-Europeans (incl. 122 Negroes, 44 West Indians, 10,846 Chinese, 2,241 Japanese), 27,031 Half-castes (incl. 20,609 Australian Aboriginals, 208 Negroes, 75 West Indians, 3,481 Chinese, 225 Japanese). The census figures do not include the full-blood Aboriginals, estimated at 60,000 (see *Statistical Year-Book of the League of Nations 1934/35*, p. 25). The population excl. full-blood Aboriginals has been estimated at 6,724,305 for 30 June 1935 (see *Quarterly Summary of Australian Statistics*, Bulletin No. 141, p. 3). We have assumed that the increase between 30 June 1933 and 30 June 1935 was confined to the full-blood Europeans.

New Zealand. According to Dominion of New Zealand *Monthly Abstract of Statistics*, Feb. 1936, p. 1, the total population excl. Maoris on 31 Dec. 1935 was 1,492,286, and incl. Maoris 1,568,220. The Maoris comprise full-blood Maoris and

APPENDIX

Maori-Europeans with at least one-half Maori blood (see New Zealand, *Population Census 1926*, vol. vi, p. 7, Wellington, 1929). According to the census of 20 April 1926 (see ibid., pp. 1, 7), the population excl. Maoris numbered 1,338,167 persons of European origin (incl. 6,053 European-Maoris with less than one-half Maori blood), 3,374 Chinese, 50 Japanese, 93 Negroes, and 2,785 other 'Race aliens'. We have assumed no change in the numbers of Chinese, &c., since 1926.

Norfolk. See *Census of Australia 1933*, Bulletin No. 8, p. 6.

Papua. Census 30 June 1933 (see *Census of Australia 1933*, Bulletin No. 5, p. 8): 1,148 full-blood Europeans, 786 full-blood non-indigenous non-Europeans (incl. 5 Chinese, 14 Japanese, 9 Negro), 227 Half-castes (incl. 7 Australian Aboriginal, 212 Papuan), 12 non-Indigenous not stated. European population, 30 June 1935: 1,229 (see *Statesman's Year-Book*, 1936, p. 423). There were in addition 274,543 Indigenous (see *The Dominions Office and Colonial Office List 1936*, p. 86).

Fiji Islands. See *Annual Colonial Reports*, No. 1719, p. 8. 'Others' include 83,289 Indians and 1,486 Chinese.

Gilbert and Ellice Islands. See *Annual Colonial Reports*, No. 1727, p. 5; *Statesman's Year-Book*, 1936, p. 444. There were 357 Asiatics.

British Solomon Islands Protectorate. See *Annual Colonial Reports*, No. 1709, p. 3.

Tonga Islands. See *Annual Colonial Reports*, No. 1724, p. 5. We have entered as Whites the 'Europeans', as Natives the 'Tongan population' and the 'Half-castes', as Others 206 'Other Pacific Islanders' and 48 'Others'.

Guam. See *Census of the United States of America 1930*, *Outlying Territories and Possessions*, pp. 291–2. Whites (1,205) include the white naval population (892). 'Others' comprise 203 Chinese, 297 Japanese, 365 Filipinos, and 37 Negroes.

Hawaii. See ibid., p. 48. 'Others' include 27,179 Chinese, 139,631 Japanese, 6,461 Koreans, 63,052 Filipinos, and 563

Negroes. Total population, 30 June 1935: 425,900 (see *Statistical Abstract of the United States 1935*, p. 10).

American Samoa. See *Census of the United States 1930, Outlying Territories*, &c., pp. 309, 311. Whites (227) include the naval personnel (178). 'Others' include 5 Chinese, 6 Japanese, and 6 Negroes.

French Settlements. Census 1 July 1931 (see *Revue d'histoire des colonies*, 1935, p. 146): 29,667 Oceanians, 5,280 French, 301 English, 169 Americans, 4,056 Chinese, 806 other nationalities and floating population. Figures do not include the population of Rapa, Rimatara, and two districts of Tuamotu (see *Résultats statistiques du recensement général de la population 1931*, vol. i, part i, p. 113).

New Caledonia. See ibid., p. 113. Whites include 658 penal population and 797 troops and sailors in the ports. There were 12,000 Asiatics.

New Hebrides. According to *Annual Colonial Reports*, No. 1681, pp. 5–6, 'some forty to sixty thousand natives and 2,318 non-natives' (969 Nationals, 50 Foreigners opted under Protocol, 42 Chinese, 29 Japanese, 1,166 Tonkinese, 62 Javanese). According to *Statistical Abstract for the British Empire 1924 to 1933*, p. 312, 31 Dec. 1933: 50,000 Natives, 1,019 Europeans, 1,299 Asiatics. *Résultats statistiques du recensement 1931*, vol. i, part i, p. 113, in 1929: 951 Europeans and Assimilated, 59,000 Natives.

Cook Island. For total population, 30 Sept. 1935, see New Zealand, *Monthly Abstract of Statistics*, Feb. 1936, p. 1. According to the census of 20 April 1926 (see New Zealand, *Population Census 1926*, vol. ii, pp. 1–2), there was a 'European' or non-native population of 313, and a 'native population' of 13,550.

Tokelau Islands. For total population, Aug. 1935, see New Zealand, *Monthly Abstract of Statistics*, Nov. 1935, p. 1. 'No Europeans reside in the islands' (New Zealand, *Population Census 1926*, vol. ii, p. 5).

APPENDIX

New Guinea. Census 30 June 1933 (see *Census of Australia 1933*, Bulletin No. 6, p. 8): 3,191 full-blood Europeans, 1,830 full-blood non-indigenous non-Europeans (incl. 1,449 Chinese, 73 Japanese), 195 Half-castes (7 Filipino, 1 Malay, 1 Maori, 8 Papuan, 178 other Polynesian). Non-indigenous population, 30 June 1935: 3,288 British, 155 Dutch, 442 Germans, 133 U.S. Americans, 1,448 Chinese, 89 Japanese, 133 Others; enumerated native population, 478,686 (see *Statesman's Year-Book*, 1936, p. 448). We have added 200,000 for the non-enumerated native population.

Nauru. Census 1 April 1935 (see *The Dominions Office and Colonial Office List 1936*, p. 224): 158 full-blood Europeans, 931 Chinese indentured labourers, 1,603 Nauruans, 4 other Pacific Islanders.

Caroline, Marianne, and Marshall Islands (Japanese Mandate). See *Financial and Economic Annual of Japan 1935*, p. 2. There were 35,328 Japanese, incl. Koreans and Formosans. We have entered all 'foreigners' as Whites.

Western Samoa. See *The Dominions Office and Colonial Office List 1936*, p. 154 (623 Europeans, 2,428 Half-castes, 50,142 Native Samoans, 503 Chinese labourers, 94 Melanesian labourers). The total population, 30 Sept. 1935, is estimated at 54,153 (see New Zealand, *Monthly Abstract of Statistics*, Feb. 1936, p. 1).

PRINTED IN
GREAT BRITAIN
AT THE
UNIVERSITY PRESS
OXFORD
BY
JOHN JOHNSON
PRINTER
TO THE
UNIVERSITY